The Influence of Librarians
in Liberal Arts Colleges
in Selected Decision Making Areas

by

George W. Whitbeck

The Scarecrow Press, Inc.
Metuchen, N. J.   1972

ISBN 0-8108-0445-X

Library of Congress Catalog Card Number 71-183945

ACKNOWLEDGMENTS

The writer is indebted to a substantial number of people for their criticism, assistance, and encouragement in the completion of this project, which is based on his Ph. D. thesis submitted to the Graduate School of Library Service at Rutgers University. First he wishes to express appreciation and thanks to his doctoral committee for their guidance and criticism throughout the development of the study. These were: Professor Ralph Blasingame (to whom, as chairman, fell the greatest burden of directing the study), Professor Ernest DeProspo, Professor Henry Voos, and the late Professor Richard Shoemaker of the Graduate School of Library Service, Rutgers University; and, Professor Bernard Goldstein, Chairman of the Sociology Department of Rutgers College. To Mr. Philip Clarke, of the Bureau of Information Science Research, an adjunct member of his committee, the writer is indebted for his assistance with the problems of data analysis. Thanks are also expressed to Dr. Lawrence Romboski, formerly of the Computer Center of Rutgers University, for his assistance in research design, and to Mr. Robert Perry and Mr. Richard Selcer, also of the Computer Center at Rutgers, for their help in data analysis.

The writer also wishes to thank the more than two hundred librarians, administrators, and faculty members at the colleges visited in the study and pretest for their time and interest.

Finally, the writer wishes to express his gratitude to Ruth, his wife, without whose patience, encouragement, and support this study might never have been completed.

Contents

LIST OF TABLES

Chapter I

INTRODUCTION

The central problem with which this study is concerned is
the role of college librarians in certain key areas of decision making in small liberal arts colleges. These areas of decision making
are: curriculum development, budgeting on both a college-wide and
a departmental level, and key staffing appointments.

In examining actual, as opposed to theoretical involvement
in curricular, budgetary, and staffing development, this study utilizes
a modification of one of the techniques applied successfully in a
classic study of influence in decision making in the political process
of a middle sized city. This study, Robert Dahl's Who Governs?,[1]
whose essential purpose is aptly described by its title, made use of
a number of data-gathering devices, among the more important of
which was that of defining a small number of key "issue areas" and
then seeking to determine what people were involved and influential
in these issues.[2] This technique, modified to allow respondents to
choose their own key issue, has been used to develop much of the
data for this study. This technique will be explained in more detail in the methodology section of this chapter and in the Appendix.

Without setting forth formal hypotheses for testing, this
study attempts to answer several questions. Some of these are as
follows. Are college librarians as involved in the development of
the curriculum of the college as are other members of the academic community (specifically, faculty members, department chairmen, and key administrators)? Are they as well informed concerning curricular change as are these other members of the academic
community? Are college librarians, at least in the sample studied,
as involved in budgetary decision-making as faculty members and
key administrators? A subsidiary, but important question is: are
the librarians as involved in the budgeting process within the

11

library as are faculty members without administrative responsibility
within their academic departments?   Concerning key appointments
at the college, are librarians involved to the same extent as faculty
members and administrators, or not?   As with budgetary decision
making, a key question in regard to appointments is the relative
involvement of librarians in appointments within the library compared with faculty involvement in appointments within their departments.   Are librarians more involved in professional appointments
in the library than are faculty members in the selection of their
colleagues?

Answers to these questions have been sought through interviews not only with librarians, but also with faculty members and
administrators.   As a consequence of interviewing members of the
latter two groups, the perceived status of academic librarians is of
some relevance to this study.   Further questions can thus be posed,
such as: what is the role of the college librarian, as perceived by
himself, by faculty members, by administrators?   Is he seen pre-
dominantly as an administrator, as a faculty member, or as a part
of neither group?   Related to this question is one concerned more
generally with the status of librarians in the college community:
that of their perceived isolation from, or their perceived integration into, this society in general.   Do faculty members, for example, see the college librarians as being more, or less, isolated
from the academic community than they are themselves?

Because of the attention given to perceived status in this
study, the findings will have some relevance to those interested in
the problem of faculty status for academic librarians.   While a
subsidiary part of the investigation, inquiry will be made into the
matter of whether or not the librarians at the institutions studied
have formal "faculty status," and if so, what benefits they have
derived from such status.   Do they have, for example, salaries
equivalent to those of faculty members?   And, are they eligible
to serve on faculty committees?   Do they have faculty titles?
Questions such as these will be treated separately from those questions concerned directly with the librarians' role in decision making, which is the main thrust of this study.   Chapter Two will be

devoted to a consideration of these questions relating to status, as
well as to certain characteristics of the population of librarians interviewed, such as age, sex, and length of service at the college.

The three areas of decision making specified as major foci of
this study were chosen as being three of the more important concerns
in the operation of an institution of higher education.   The development of curriculum is certainly a vital concern of the faculty and
administration, and in view of the interest of academic librarians in
the achievement of faculty status and in involving the library in the
learning process, it would seem logical that it should be an equally
vital concern for them.   Budgeting, the allocation of scarce resources, is obviously another vitally important topic without which
the study of any group's role in decision making would be incom-
plete.   The outcome of the decision-making process in budgeting is
frequently the key to what can be done in other areas.   The role of
the librarians in important appointments at the college level is seen
as another touchstone of the relative degree of influence of librarians in the college.   Appointments are another area vital to the
carrying out of the goals of the college.

Chapters three through five are devoted to the presentation
and explication of data obtained in this study relevant to the role of
the librarians in decision making in curriculum, budgeting, and staffing.

Chapter III, specifically, considers the relationship of the
librarians to the decision-making process in development of the curriculum at the college.   This chapter looks first at the data accumulated in the open-end questions relating to the curricular issues cited
as having been important at the college in recent years.   These data are approached from both an overall and a specific view.   That
is, a comparison is first made of the total number of aspects of an
issue discussed by the different classes of respondents.   Then, significant points in regard to particular aspects of issues are considered.   The data accumulated in the more direct questioning concerning the respondent's relationship to curriculum development are then
detailed.   A consideration of these findings by sample strata com-
pletes this chapter.

Chapter IV covers the relationship of the librarians to budgetary decision making, and is organized in much the same way as
Chapter III.   Chapter V considers the role of the librarians in key
appointments at the college, and likewise proceeds from general to
specific data.   Some attention is paid in both Chapter IV and Chapter V to a comparison of the relative degree of influence in decision making in budgeting and appointments within the department (or
the library) of faculty members and librarians.

Related Literature

The relationship of the library and librarians to the academic institution of which they are a part has been a subject of interest, even a preoccupation, of the profession for many years. Apart
from works devoted primarily to "how-to-do" the job of providing
library service to institutions of higher education,[3] there have been
a substantial number of writings which, while not entirely neglect-
ing the "how-to" of academic library service, have concerned themselves to a very great degree with such questions as: what sorts
of jobs the library should be doing and, further, what the role, or
status, of the librarians should be.

This preoccupation with what the academic library should be
doing and what its relationship should be to the college or university of which it is a part (these seem to be opposite sides of the
same coin) received perhaps its classic statement in Harvie Branscomb's Teaching with Books, an eclectic work dealing with many
aspects of the library-university interface.   Based on a number of
research studies done in the 1930's, Branscomb chided academic
libraries for their isolation and preoccupation with techniques to the
neglect of service.[4]

More recently, Knapp studied in some detail an attempt to
involve the library more closely in the development of the curriculum of a college than is ordinarily the case.[5]   In order to attempt
this experiment, Knapp and her colleagues examined the social
structure of Monteith College, looking at the relationship between
the three "models" existing in the college (bureaucracy, collegial,

and "free and independent teacher"). A key finding of Knapp's was that the library occupied a distinctly peripheral position in the social structure of the college.

Knapp has also contributed an exploratory survey article, "The College Librarian: Sociology of a Professional Specialization,"[6] in which she called for greater study of the relationship of college librarians to their sociological environment.

Another writer who has concerned himself with this problem is Daniel P. Bergen. In addition to co-editing (with E.D. Duryea) a valuable collection of essays entitled Librarians and the College Climate of Learning,[7] Bergen has contributed a number of controversial and insightful articles on this problem. Bergen suggests that "... librarians and teachers belong to different, often mutually exclusive sub-cultures within the collegiate setting."[8] He contrasts the "disciplinary cosmopolitans" among the faculty, who have as their reference group fellow scholar-researchers in their subject area, with the locally and bureaucratically oriented librarians.

One solution to the problem of faculty-librarian relations is that of the "library-college" movement, concerning which much has been written in recent years. While this term means different things to different people, essentially the library-college idea involves the absorption of librarians into the faculty, or vice versa, with this combined group being freed from "publish or perish" pressures and the mundane tasks of cataloging or circulating books and able to devote full time to the education of undergraduate students.[9] An indication of the reception that such far-reaching innovation can perhaps expect to receive is shown by comments taken from Swarthmore College's Critique of a College.[10] This careful study of the relationship of the library to the college at Swarthmore, while paying tribute to the "nobility of purpose" of library-college advocates, criticizes the program as involving so heavy an involvement in the curriculum by the library that it "tends to overwhelm the discipline-oriented system, justifiably arousing faculty resentment."[11] This reaction, at one of the most highly esteemed liberal arts colleges in the country, appears to be in line with Jencks and Riesman's

thesis that the academic professionals increasingly control undergraduate education in the United States, a development that would
appear to be most inauspicious for any program such as the "library-college."[12]

Several doctoral dissertations have either directly attacked
the problem of librarian-college (faculty, administration) relations
or have shed light on the subject. In one, Joseph N. Whitten surveyed, by questionnaire or interview, seventy-two head librarians,
fifty-three faculty members, and fifty-three administrators with a
view to describing "how a library may become an integral and func-
tional part of the academic program and planning of the college."[13]
Whitten concluded that the basic claim of the librarian to "pedagog-
ical responsibility" lay in the practice of his profession, and that
librarians have underrated the possibilities for involvement in academic affairs.

Henry H. Scherer conducted a broad survey of faculty-li-
brary relations on two hundred and seventy-five liberal arts campuses, seeking to answer the question: "How well do the faculty
member and the librarian on the liberal arts college campus work
together in gathering and using library materials?"[14] Scherer
found, at least in this limited sphere, that faculty-librarian relations were remarkably good. While this finding might be considered
encouraging to academic librarians, it appears to fly in the face of
the results of other studies of academic libraries that have been
mentioned. It may be suspected that Scherer's reliance upon the
questionnaire as his source of data, plus the small number of returns from each campus chosen for his sample (he received 1,197
replies from 275 colleges), may have resulted in his receiving a
superficial picture.

Another dissertation somewhat related to this problem, although confined to examining public community colleges, is that of
Donald Meyer. One significant finding related to the present study
is the contrast Meyer reported between the desire of faculty members for a semi-decentralized library and that of the librarians for
a centralized facility.[15]

Another dissertation which may be of great use in understanding the dynamics of academic librarianship is that of Kenneth
H. Plate.   Plate's proposed model of library middle management
personnel, although based upon data obtained from large university
libraries, may well provide insights into the role and status of librarians in other academic libraries, at least in the case of the
chief librarians. [16]

Two other studies relating to college librarians should be
mentioned.   One is Anita Schiller's Characteristics of Professional
Personnel in College and University Libraries, [17] a study of such
factors as vital statistics, educational background, salaries, and
also what academic librarians think of their careers.   The other is
Perry Morrison's monumental study of The Career of the Academic
Librarian, [18] in which he covered such topics as the background of
academic librarians, their education, and their psychological characteristics.   Both of these works provide valuable background to
the present study.

Methodology of the Study [19]

The sample of colleges for study in this investigation was
chosen randomly from a population consisting of private liberal arts
colleges in the states of New Jersey, New York, and Pennsylvania
having an enrollment of between eight hundred and two thousand students.   The sampling was stratified to ensure that colleges with
relatively well supported libraries and those with poorly supported
libraries would both be included.   Average annual expenditure, per
student, on the library (averaged over a period of five years, 1963
to 1968) was used as a measure to rank and stratify the population
of colleges.

Personal interviews, most of which lasted for from thirty
to forty-five minutes, were used to collect the vast bulk of data for
this study.   A short preliminary questionnaire directed to the chief
librarians was also used for supplemental statistical data.

Interviews were conducted, at each of the ten colleges chosen, with the following personnel: the academic dean, the chief

fiscal officer (business manager, or treasurer), three or four professional librarians (including the chief librarian and a representa-
tive of readers' services and one of technical services), four department chairmen, and at least ten percent of the faculty. The
faculty respondents, and the sample of department chairmen, were
both chosen by stratified random sampling in order to assure rep-
resentation of various disciplinary sub-divisions of the faculty. Interviewing was conducted during the spring of 1969.

Notes

1. Robert A. Dahl, Who Governs? Democracy and Power in an
    American City (New Haven: Yale University Press, 1961).

2. Ibid., p. 331.

3. See, for example, William M. Randall and Francis Goodrich,
    Principles of College Library Administration (Chicago:
    University of Chicago Press, 1936); Guy R. Lyle, Admin-
    istration of the College Library (3rd ed.; New York: H.W.
    Wilson Co., 1961); and Louis R. Wilson and Maurice F.
    Tauber, The University Library (New York: Columbia Uni-
    versity Press, 1956), to mention only a few.

4. Harvie Branscomb, Teaching with Books: A Study of College
    Libraries (Hamden, Conn.: The Shoe String Press, Inc.,
    1964).

5. Patricia B. Knapp, The Monteith College Library Experiment
    (New York: The Scarecrow Press, Inc., 1966).

6. In The Status of American College and University Librarians,
    ed. by Robert R. Downs, ACRL Monograph No. 22 (Chi-
    cago: American Library Association, 1958), p. 56-65.

7. Daniel P. Bergen and E.D. Duryea, Librarians and the Col-
    lege Climate of Learning (Syracuse: Syracuse University
    Press, 1964).

8. Daniel P. Bergen, "Librarians and the Bipolarization of the
    Academic Enterprise," College and Research Libraries,
    XXIV (November, 1963), 467.

9. See Robert T. Jordan, "The Library-College: A Merging of
    Library and Classroom," in Bergen and Duryea, op. cit.,
    p. 37-60.

10. Swarthmore College, Critique of a College, Reports of the

Commission on Educational Policy, the Special Committee on Library Policy, and the Special Committee on Student Life (Swarthmore, Pa.: Swarthmore College, 1967).

11. Ibid., p. 338.

12. See Christopher Jencks and David Riesman, The Academic Revolution (Garden City, N.Y.: Doubleday, 1969).

13. Joseph N. Whitten, "The Relationship of College Instruction to Libraries in 72 Liberal Arts Colleges" (unpublished Ed. D. dissertation, New York University, 1958).

14. Henry H. Scherer, "Faculty-Librarian Relationships in Selected Liberal Arts Colleges" (unpublished Ed. D. dissertation, University of Southern California, 1960), p. 10.

15. See Donald P. Meyer, "An Investigation of Perceptions Regarding the Instructional Function of the Library Among Faculty Members and Librarians at Public Community Colleges in Michigan" (unpublished Ph. D. dissertation, University of Michigan, 1968).

16. Plate, Kenneth Harry, "Middle Management in University Libraries: the Development of a Theoretical Model for Analysis" (Unpublished Ph. D. dissertation, Rutgers University, 1969).

17. Anita Schiller, Characteristics of Professional Personnel in College and University Libraries (Springfield: Illinois State Library, 1969).

18. Perry D. Morrison, The Career of the Academic Librarian: A Study of the Social Origins, Educational Attainments, Vocational Experience, and Personality Characteristics of a Group of American Librarians (Chicago: American Library Association, 1969).

19. A more detailed statement of the methodology of this study will be found in the Appendix.

Chapter II

THE COLLEGE LIBRARIAN IN THE ACADEMIC COMMUNITY

This chapter is devoted to the discussion of a number of general factors related to the role of college librarians in the academic community. These are: the role of the college librarians as perceived both by faculty members and administrators, and by the librarians themselves; the relative degree of librarians' isolation from the rest of the academic community, as perceived by faculty members and administrators; the closest contacts of the librarians in the college; the specific reasons for librarian-faculty and librarian-administrator contact; and, the relationship of the librarians to the committee structure of the college. These variables provide an overall view of the role of the librarian in the college community which supplements the findings of the following chapters relating to specific aspects of decision making in the college; and, to some degree, they may also explain those findings. That is, the perceptions of referent groups may influence the role the librarians can play in decision making in the college.

Before looking at these variables, however, some acquaintance with a number of characteristics of the sampling of librarians studied is in order. All librarian respondents were questioned as to such general variables as age, length of service at the college, education, whether or not they had faculty status, etc., and some consideration of these data may serve as an introduction and background to discussion of the perceived status of librarians in the college and their role in decision making.

Education

Of the thirty-one librarians interviewed at the ten colleges studied, twenty-four held the professional master's degree in librarianship; and, in almost all cases, this degree had been obtained

20

from a library school accredited by the American Library Association. To a considerable extent, the librarians represented in the sample tended to be local people who had gone to the closest ALA-accredited school for their professional training.

Age

The librarians serving in small liberal arts colleges tend to be an older group of people, by and large, if the findings of this study can be generalized to any appreciable degree. Twenty-one of the thirty-one interviewed were over the age of fifty (nine of these were over sixty), and twenty-five of the thirty-one were over forty. Only two librarians were aged thirty or under.

Sex

Some note should be made of the sex distribution of the population of librarians studied, although no statistical correlation was noted between sex and any of the dependent variables examined. Of the thirty-one librarians interviewed, eleven were men. Of these eleven, eight were chief librarians, one was the chief of technical services for his library, and the other two were reference librarians.

Marital Status

The majority of the librarians in the study, twenty-one out of thirty-one, were married. Nine were single, and one was divorced.

Length of Service at the College

One other variable is important to fill out the picture of the college librarians interviewed in this study, namely the length of time in service at the college. Here wide variety was encountered, with the preponderance of the population having a relatively short tenure. Twenty of the thirty-one had been at the college seven years or less. Only four of the librarians had been at the college more than fifteen years, and two more had served from twelve to fifteen years.

Faculty Status

Although, as mentioned earlier, this study does not deal primar-
ly with the problem of faculty status for academic librarians, this topic
was considered relevant enough to warrant collecting some data on the
subject. All librarians interviewed were asked a short sequence of
questions relating to their situation in regard to faculty status.
They were asked whether or not they had faculty status; then,
whether certain attributes usually considered to be a part of faculty
status applied to their situation. These questions were: whether
the librarians enjoyed faculty titles; whether they had a nine- or
ten-month (i.e., faculty) contract; whether they had the right to
vote at faculty meetings; whether they were eligible for sabbatical
leave; whether or not they had to meet faculty requirements for appointment; whether or not their salary scales were equivalent to
those of the faculty; whether they were covered by faculty retirement provisions; and, whether or not they were eligible for mem-
bership on faculty committees.

These questions produced several interesting results. In the
first place, the responses to three questions were extremely one-
sided: none of the librarians interviewed had a nine- or ten-month
contract (i.e., were obligated to the same amount of work as faculty members, or were compensated for the extra month or two of
work that they put in); almost none of the librarians had to meet
faculty requirements for appointment; and, all librarians were eligible for faculty retirement programs.

Returning to the preliminary question, that of whether or
not the librarians felt that they had, or had been told that they had
faculty status, it is interesting to note that twenty-seven of the
thirty-one stated that they did have faculty status.

Twenty librarians responded that they did have faculty titles.
That is, they held the title of associate professor, or assistant
professor, etc. The other eleven did not have these titles.

Twenty-three of the thirty-one stated that they did not have
salaries equivalent to faculty members; five stated that they did,
and the other three responded that they really didn't know if their

Table 1

Faculty Status and Its Attributes

Question	Yes	No	Don't Know
Have Faculty Status?	25	6	
Have Faculty Contract (9 or 10 month with compensation for summer)?	0	31	
Must Meet Faculty Standards for Appointment?	3	28	
Have Salaries Equivelant to Faculty?	5	23	3
Have Faculty Titles?	20	11	
Have right to vote at Faculty Meetings?	25	6	
Have Sabbatical Leave Privilege?	15	11	5
Eligible for Service on Faculty Committees?	23	8	

salaries were equal to faculty members with equivalent rank, service, etc.

The response to the question relating to whether or not the librarians had the privilege of voting at faculty meetings broke down as follows: twenty-five had this right, and six did not.

The question of eligibility for sabbatical leave produced a rather confused picture. Eleven of the librarians stated that they did not have this privilege; fifteen said that they did, while five frankly said that they didn't know if they were eligible for sabbatical leave privileges or not.

The vast majority of librarians interviewed, twenty-three out of the thirty-one, to be exact, stated that they were eligible for service on faculty committees. Table 1 shows these results in tabular form.

Summary

Briefly summarizing, the population of librarians interviewed in this study exhibits the following characteristics: most (twenty-five out of thirty-one) have a professional master's degree from an accredited library school; they are an older group of people (twen-

ty-one out of thirty-one are over fifty); most (twenty of thirty-one)
are women, but the men hold down all but two of the chief librarians' positions; most (twenty-one of thirty-one) are married; and
most of them (twenty of thirty-one) have a relatively short tenure
at the college they serve.   In regard to variables generally assumed to relate to faculty status, the data achieved in these interviews is somewhat contradictory.   (This fact will not be a surprise
to those familiar with academic libraries.)   Most of those interviewed stated that they had faculty status, and the majority had
faculty titles.   All were included in the faculty retirement plan.
On the other hand, no librarian had a faculty contract, in terms of
service obligation, and very few could claim that they had salaries
equal to those of faculty members.   The opportunity to take sabbatical leave was apparently available to fifteen of the thirty-one librarians interviewed, and the vast majority considered themselves
eligible to serve on faculty committees.

The Librarians in the Committee Structure of the College

        Although the majority of librarians in this study indicated
that they were eligible for service on faculty committees, very few
of them have been given the opportunity (or have availed themselves
of the opportunity) to serve their institutions in this capacity.   Of
the thirty-one librarians interviewed, only fourteen held committee
appointments.   There were actually sixteen committee appointments
held by the librarians, but this was due to the fact that two librarians held double appointments.[1]   Of these sixteen committee assignments, nine were to the Library Committee of the college.   And,
six of the sixteen memberships were found at one college (Geneva
College).   Table 2 shows the committees of which the librarians
were members.

        One question arising from this data relates to the relative
importance of these bodies of which the librarians are members.
Are these committees recognized as being among the more influential on campus, or not?   To attack this problem, all respondents,
faculty members and administrators as well as librarians, were

Table 2

Librarian Committee Memberships

Committee	No. Serving	College(s)
Library Committee	9	Waynesburg, Thiel, Bloomfield, Geneva (2 members), Ursinus (2 members), Lycoming, Hamilton
Curriculum Study Committee	1	Thiel
Academic Policy Committee	1	Dickinson
Promotion of Academic Achievement	1	Geneva
Foreign Student Advisory Committee	1	Geneva
Spiritual Activities Committee	1	Geneva
Freshman Orientation Committee	1	Geneva
Memorial Room Committee	1	Hamilton

asked to cite what they considered to be the most important and influential committees at their college. In no case was the Library Committee cited as the "most important," or "most influential" committee, although it was cited as "important" by library--conscious faculty members on a few occasions. Only at Thiel College, where the chief librarian was a member of the Curriculum Study Committee, and at Dickinson College, where the chief librarian served on the Academic Policy Committee, was a librarian a member of a committee cited as "most important and influential" by any member of the academic community at that college.

In general, then, it would appear that college librarians, at least in the population studied, play only a very minor role in the committee structure of their institutions. Only a minority of the librarians (after allowance is made for multiple memberships),

serve at all and except for two cases, their service is on committees considered of secondary rank in terms of importance and influence. The Library Committee of the college is almost invariably
considered to be in this category.

Other Contacts of Librarians with the College Community

In order to fill out the sociological portrait of the college li
brarian obtained in the main thrust of this investigation, that is,
his role in curricular, budgetary, and staffing decision-making, all
respondents were asked specifically to cite their closest professional
contacts at the college. While no strong conclusions may be based
upon this particular bit of survey data (for one thing, "contact" was
not precisely defined; therefore, one person's contacts are not nec-
essarily the equivalent of another's), some description of the cited
contacts of the college librarians interviewed may be of interest.

Table 3

Professional Contacts of Librarians**

Librarians	Disciplinary Strata					Total
	Hum.	S. S.	N. S.	(D. C.)	(Fac.)	
Chief Librarians	10	14	10	(21)	(13)	34
Reader Services Librarians	18	20	4	(15)	(27)	42
Technical Services Libns.	13	12	5	(12)	(18)	30
TOTAL	41(38%)	46(43%)	19(19%)	(48)	(58)	106

**Abbreviations used: Hum. - Members of Humanities Departments;
S. S. - Members of Social Science Departments; N. S. - Members of Na
tural Science Departments; D. C. - Department Chairmen; Fac. - Regu
lar Faculty

Table 3 shows, in composite form, the classes of faculty members cited as being the closest professional contacts of the librarians.
It is apparent that the contacts of college librarians, as cited by themselves, are random, at least in regard to the subject area of the
faculty member. When one notes, however, that the Humanities[2]
faculty is usually a much larger proportion of the whole faculty at

the small liberal arts colleges studied than is the faculty of social sciences, it is perhaps of interest that both the chief librarians and the reader services librarians cited more contact with the latter than with the former.[3] As might be expected, only the chief librarians cited more contacts with department chairmen than with other faculty members.

The most significant fact about the professional contacts between college librarians and faculty members, however, is their infrequency. When one considers the responses of faculty members concerning the frequency of their contact with any librarian, as well as the responses of the librarians concerning their faculty contacts, one finds that of this combined population, sixty-eight percent saw each other only once a month, or less. This figure could hardly be considered encouraging by advocates of a more involved role for the library in the educational work of the college.

Specific Service Most Frequently Performed by Librarians

Related to the above findings are those on the actual tasks that the librarians most frequently perform in giving service to faculty members. All librarians and faculty members were queried, not only concerning the frequency of their contacts with faculty (librarians in the case of faculty members), but also as to the reasons for their contacts. Far and away the most frequent reason cited for faculty-librarian contact was "collection building," consultation regarding orders for books, periodicals, or other materials. Sixty-three percent of the 163 librarians and faculty members interviewed (here including department chairmen) cited this reason. Using, or giving, reference service and consultation regarding the reserve book collection were poor seconds as reasons for librarian-faculty contact, with only 19 percent of the interviewees citing them.

Regarding contact with administrators, as might be expected, only the chief librarian had contact with either the academic dean or the chief fiscal officer more frequently than once a month.

Table 4

Perceived Isolation of Librarians

	Considerably more isolated	Somewhat more isolated	Same contact	Somewhat less isolated	Considerably less isolated	Total
Faculty members	26 (28%)	25 (27%)	37 (40%)	3 (3%)	1 (1%)	92
Department chairmen and academic deans	8 (16%)	19 (38%)	21 (42%)	2 (4%)	0 (0%)	50
Fiscal officers	4 (40%)	2 (20%)	4 (40%)	0 (0%)	0 (0%)	10
TOTAL	38 (25%)	46 (30%)	62 (41%)	5 (3%)	1 (1%)	152

Respondents' Perceptions of the Relative
Degree of Isolation of the Librarians

Another interesting and possibly significant variable which was tested is the degree to which faculty members and administrators perceive librarians as being isolated from the rest of the college. It was presumed that the relative degree of isolation of the librarians would be somewhat related to their role, or lack of one, in decision making.

Table 4 shows the distribution of response to the above questions. Eighty-four, or 55 percent of the respondents, cited the librarians as being more isolated "than the members of the average faculty department." Another 41 percent felt the librarians were no more isolated than the "members of the average faculty department."[4] Only six interviewees felt that the library staff was less isolated than faculty department members. There is no statistically significant relationship between the perceptions of faculty members and administrators in regard to this question.

Perceptions of the Role of College Librarians:
Faculty, Administrative, or Separate Group?

Perhaps the most useful of the questions relating to the librarian's status in general are those on their perceived role in the college. All librarian respondents were asked whether they felt that they were looked upon by faculty members and administrators as a part of the administration or as a part of the faculty. They were then asked how they themselves perceived their role. Table 5 shows the distribution resulting from these questions. It is interesting to note that fifteen out of the thirty-one librarians interviewed (48%) felt they were looked upon by faculty and administrators as being more a part of the administration than the faculty. On the other hand, six out of the thirty-one responded that they were "more a part of the faculty than administration" (none stated that they were seen as "part of faculty"), and three more answered that they were "part of both groups." Seven, or 23 percent, of the librarians felt they were seen as part of neither faculty nor admin-

Table 5

Comparison of Librarians' Own Perceptions of Their Role
with Their Feelings As to How They Are
Perceived by Others

Librarians' own perceptions of their role	Librarians' feelings as to how they are perceived by others				
	Administration	Neither	Both	Faculty	Total
Administration, or more administration than faculty	6				6 (19%)
Neither group	5	3		1	9 (29%)
Both groups	2		2		4 (13%)
Faculty, or more faculty than administration	2	4	1	5	12 (39%)
TOTAL	15 (48%)	7 (23%)	3 (10%)	6 (19%)	31 (100%)

istration. While conclusions based on so small a number of respondents must be highly tentative, it is perhaps noteworthy that
such a large percentage of librarians (71%) feel that they are seen
by these two significant referent groups (faculty and administrators)
as being either part of the bureaucratic administrative structure or
as being a separate group.

On the other hand, when the librarians were asked what they
felt about their role, whether they saw it as placing them with administration, faculty, or with neither group, there was a swing to
the faculty side of the scale. Twelve (39%) felt that they were
either faculty, or closer to the faculty than to the administration;
four others felt they were part of both groups. Nine respondents
felt they were a separate group, while only six placed themselves
with the administration. On the basis of this limited sample, it

would appear that at least some of the librarians in liberal arts colleges identify with the faculty, but that they feel that they are not accepted in this role by others.   No statistically significant differences were found between the responses of the various types of librarians (chief librarians, reader services librarians, and technical services librarians) to these questions.

In order to obtain the actual feelings of nonlibrarians as to the librarian's role, all faculty and administration respondents were asked to place the librarians in one of the same categories utilized above.   In general, it would appear that the faculty members and administrators saw the role of the librarians as being far closer to that visualized by the librarians themselves, for themselves, than to the role some librarians felt was ascribed to them.   For example, 47 percent of faculty and administrators interviewed placed the librarians as being either in the "faculty" or "more a part of part of faculty than administration" categories, where 39 percent of the librarians themselves had done this.   Twenty-two percent of non-librarians responded that the librarians belonged with the administrators (categories one and two), compared to 19 percent of librarians.   The proportion of faculty and administrators describing the librarians as being part of "neither group" was almost exactly the same as the proportion of librarians.   There were no significant differences among the perceptions of faculty members, department chairmen and academic deans, and the fiscal officers (See Table 6).

In order to determine whether or not the faculty and administrators saw the chief librarian as having a distinctively different status than that of staff librarians, these respondents were queried as to this matter.   One hundred and twenty, or 79 percent, answered that they would make no distinction between the role of the chief librarian and other librarians.   The remainder were about equally divided as to whether the chief librarian was more of an administrator, or more a part of the faculty, than the staff librarians.   See Table 7 for the distribution of these responses.

Table 6

Faculty and Administrator Perceptions of Librarians' Role

	Administration	More administration than faculty	Neither group	Both groups	More faculty than administration	Faculty	Total
Faculty members	6 (7%)	15 (16%)	24 (26%)	2 (2%)	38 (41%)	7 (8%)	92
Department chairmen and academic deans	2 (4%)	7 (14%)	17 (34%)	2 (4%)	18 (36%)	4 (8%)	50
Fiscal officers	1 (10%)	2 (20%)	3 (30%)	1 (10%)	1 (10%)	2 (20%)	10
TOTAL	9 (6%)	24 (16%)	44 (29%)	5 (3%)	57 (38%)	13 (9%)	152

Note: Percentage total of 101 occurs due to rounding.

Table 7

Perceived Role of the Chief Librarian, As Distinguished from Staff Librarians

	No distinction made	Chief librarian more of an administrator	Chief librarian more of a faculty member	"Other"	Total
Faculty members	76 (83%)	7 (8%)	7 (8%)	2 (2%)	92
Department chairmen and academic deans	38 (76%)	4 (8%)	5 (10%)	3 (6%)	50
Fiscal officers	6 (60%)	2 (20%)	1 (10%)	1 (10%)	10
TOTAL	120 (79%)	13 (9%)	13 (9%)	6 (4%)	152

Note: Percentage total of 101 occurs due to rounding.

Perceptions of the Quality of Campus Communication

Related to the perceptions of respondents concerning the isolation of various academic departments are their perceptions of the
quality of communication at the college.   It was assumed that their
view of the quality of communication would be related to their participation in decision making at the college.   All interviewees were
asked to express an opinion concerning communication at the college
both between departments and between the administration and the
various departments.   Tables 8 and 9 show the compressed (both as
to class of respondent and response variables) distribution of responses to these questions.   There is no statistically significant difference between the responses of librarians and those of other interviewees.   Evidently most interviewees are satisfied with the state
of communication at their institutions, as approximately half of the
respondents described communication as excellent or good, while
only 15 percent (roughly), in both variables, described them as poor
or very bad.   A higher percentage of librarians than others described communication as poor or bad (26% in interdepartmental
communication and 23% in communication between administration and
departments), but, as stated above, the statistics computed for both
variables show this difference to be insignificant.

Summary

This chapter has been devoted to a consideration of a number of variables related basically to the status of librarians in small
liberal arts colleges.   First, a number of variables relating to the
sample of librarians interviewed were considered, among them age,
sex, faculty status, academic titles, and salaries equivalent to those
of faculty members.

Regarding the librarians' role, actual or perceived, in the
society of the college, it was seen that they have only a minimal
role in the committee structure of the college.   Responses to questioning related to the closest professional contacts of the librarians
showed that these contacts were random in nature as between the
various disciplinary subdivisions of the faculty.   The most frequent

Table 8

Perceived Quality of Communication Between Departments

	Good-excellent	Fair	Poor, very bad	Total
Librarians	11 (36%)	12 (39%)	8 (26%)	31
Faculty members	44 (48%)	35 (38%)	13 (14%)	92
Department chairmen and academic deans	30 (60%)	14 (28%)	6 (12%)	50
Fiscal officers	5 (50%)	4 (40%)	1 (10%)	10
TOTAL	90 (49%)	65 (36%)	28 (15%)	183

Table 9

Perceived Quality of Communication Between the Administration and the Academic Departments

	Good-excellent	Fair	Poor, very bad	Total
Librarians	12 (39%)	12 (39%)	7 (23%)	31
Faculty members	43 (47%)	34 (37%)	15 (16%)	92
Department chairmen and academic deans	32 (64%)	12 (24%)	6 (12%)	50
Fiscal officers	5 (50%)	4 (40%)	1 (10%)	10
TOTAL	92 (50%)	62 (34%)	29 (16%)	183

reasons for contact between faculty and librarians was collection building.

In regard to the degree of isolation of the librarians from the rest of the college (relative to faculty departments), a majority of faculty and administrative respondents felt that the librarians were more isolated than the members of the average faculty department. Only a very small number of respondents (6) felt that the librarians were less isolated than faculty members.

In regard to the perceived role of the librarians, it was found that the librarians' own perception of their role tended to be quite close to what faculty members and administrators perceived it to be. Thirty-nine percent of librarians interviewed stated that their role was primarily that of a faculty member, while another 13 percent saw themselves as being a part of both the faculty and administrative groups. Forty-six percent of faculty members and administrators saw the librarians as being faculty members, with another three percent seeing them as having a foot in both camps. However, some librarians tended to feel that they were not accepted in a faculty role, as witnessed by the fact that only 19 percent of them felt that they were accepted in a faculty role by others.

All respondents were questioned concerning their perceptions of the adequacy of communication on the campus. No statistically significant differences were found in responses to this questioning between classes of interviewees, although the librarians tended to take a slightly dimmer view of campus communication than faculty members and administrators. Twenty-six percent of librarians considered communication between departments to be poor, as opposed to 14 percent of faculty members and 12 percent of academic deans and department chairmen.

Notes

1. The chief librarian at Hamilton College was serving on both the Library Committee and the Memorial Room Committee; the chief librarian at Thiel College was a member of both the Library Committee and the Curriculum Study Committee.

2. The following course-offering departments were included in the

faculty sub-division "Humanities": Classics, English, Fine
Arts, Foreign Languages, Music, Philosophy, Physical Edu-
cation, Religion, and Speech (Drama). Those departments
included in the category "Social Sciences" were: Business
Administration, Economics, Education, History, Political
Science, Psychology, and Sociology (Anthropology). Those
classed in the category "Natural Sciences" were: Biology,
Chemistry, Geology, Mathematics, Physics, and Engineering.
This classification, while admittedly somewhat arbitrary,
was adhered to systematically throughout the investigation.

3. In regard to particular departments cited, history faculty were
most frequently cited as close contacts by chief librarians
and reader services people; foreign language faculty were
most often cited by technical service personnel. Obviously,
no statistical significance may be drawn from this data due
to the relatively small numbers involved.

4. It is important to note that faculty and administration interviewees were asked to compare the degree of isolation of the librarians with that of members of faculty departments, and
not merely to consider the librarians as a distinct group.
It is likely, but problematic, that the large number of respondents who felt that the librarians were no more isolated
than faculty members is due to recognition on the part of
some respondents that many faculty members are themselves
somewhat isolated.

Chapter III

THE ROLE OF COLLEGE LIBRARIANS IN THE
DEVELOPMENT OF CURRICULUM

This chapter is devoted to a consideration of the librarians' role in key decisions relating to the development of curriculum at the colleges surveyed. The teaching role of college librarians, and the need for their involvement in the curriculum of the college has been a subject of great interest to academic librarians for many years. This chapter presents a picture of what this relationship actually is at the ten small liberal arts colleges examined in this study.

A variety of approaches were used to develop the picture of the college librarians' role in curriculum development. First, an attempt was made to develop a picture of the trends in curriculum revision at the college in the past two or three years (as well as the interviewee's knowledge of these trends) through a series of questions related to what the respondent considered to be the one or two most important curricular issues to come up at the college in this period.

Tables 10 through 19 show the issues cited at each of the ten colleges, together with the number of persons in each general class citing each issue as either the most important or next most important to come up at the college in recent years. The number cited ranges from five to thirteen. In general, those colleges where fewer issues were cited are those at which some major curricular change had taken place in recent years which stood out in the minds of most respondents; at the others, either no outstanding change had occurred or change had been gradual.

In no case was there a significant relationship between the class of the respondent (librarian, faculty member, administrator) and the curricular issues cited. The tables listing the issues are

(cont. p. 49)

Table 10

Curricular Issues Cited--Hamilton College)

Issue	Cited by		
	Librar-ians	Faculty members	Department chairmen and aca-demic deans
I. Major revision (1967-1968) of curriculum: included calendar change (to 4-1-4 Plan) and abolition of fixed distribution requirements for graduation	3	9	5
II. Revision of Chemistry Department courses		1	
III. Transition to Cluster College concept (founding of coordinate women's college: Kirkland College)			1
IV. Pass-fail grading system: should it be instituted, and to what extent?		1	
V. Black Studies Cultural Center		1	

Table 11

Curricular Issues Cited--Dickinson College

Issue	Cited by		
	Librarians	Faculty members	Department chairmen and academic deans
I. Consideration of calendar change (from semester to 4-1-4 or some other option)		2	1
II. Revision of distribution and other graduation requirements	1	3	4
III. ROTC (should academic credit be given for its courses, should it be allowed on campus, etc.?)	1	2	
IV. Course revision in particular departments; strengthening major sequences, etc.	1	3	
V. Grading system: should pass-fail option be granted, and if so, to what extent?	1	1	1
VI. Underclass educational experience (freshmen and sophomores); development of interdisciplinary courses for this level		4	
VII. Inordinate and undue expansion of curriculum		1	
VIII. Independent study; honors projects by students	1	2	2
IX. Clash between classical liberal arts and "useful" knowledge		1	
X. How far should the college go in serving the community, i.e., in offering courses designed to meet the needs of local industry, schools, government, etc.?		1	
XI. Student involvement in curricular change		2	

Table 12

Curricular Issues Cited--Thiel College

| | Cited by | | |
Issue	Librar-ians	Faculty members	Department chairmen and aca-demic deans
I. Calendar change: should it be changed from semester to some other type? Reduction of course load also involved in this.	2	7	5
II. Requirements for majors, both general college and departmental		3	2
III. Setting up of new Music Education program for prospective music teachers	1		
IV. Comprehensive exams for students: should they be abolished, or revised?		4	
V. Should the college drop certain business and secretarial courses?		1	
VI. Development of interdisciplinary courses		1	1
VII. Should academic credit be given for certain student activities?			1
VIII. Reemphasis of teacher education program			1
IX. Team teaching in some courses, specifically general biology		1	
X. Academic freedom: freedom to engage in political activities without fear of reprisal		1	
XI. Expansion of Art Department and its program	1		

Table 13

Curricular Issues Cited--Bloomfield College

Issue	Cited by		
	Librarians	Faculty members	Department chairmen and academic deans
I. Cooperative education program (internship, job experience as part of academic program)	1	3	4
II. Push for a more flexible curriculum, generally		1	1
III. Student membership on faculty committees	1	1	
IV. Introduction of black studies into curriculum	1	3	
V. Need to develop more interdepartmental courses		1	
VI. Expansion of Spanish Department course offerings		1	
VII. Introduction of Nursing Program			1
VIII. Introduction of computer science course in Business Administration curriculum		1	
IX. Coordinated Freshman Studies (interdisciplinary courses set up for freshmen)		2	
X. Condensation of some two-semester courses to one semester			1
XI. Should the major in Physics be dropped?			1
XII. Urban Studies Program: should it be instituted?			1
XIII. Process of curricular change itself	1		

Table 14

Curricular Issues Cited--Lycoming College

| | Cited by | | |
| | | | |
Issue	Librar- ians	Faculty members	Department chairmen and aca- demic deans
I. Lycoming Plan (con- sisted of a substantial calendar change plus changes in teaching methods)	3	8	5
II. Academic freedom (interpreted as freedom to teach what, where, and how the instructor desires)		1	
III. Four-course load (per semester)		1	2
IV. College Scholar Pro- gram (independent study for top-rated students)		1	
V. Western Thought Course (interdisciplinary course)			1

Table 15

Curricular Issues Cited--Elizabethtown College

	Cited by		
Issue	Librar-ians	Faculty members	Department chairmen and aca-demic deans
I. Professionalism versus the Liberal Arts (i.e., tension between emphasis of these two trends in the curriculum of the school)			1
II. Revamping offerings of the Education Department	3	1	1
III. Debate over the Remedial English course (whether there should be one or not)	1	4	2
IV. Direction of the General Education Program; what should be the core curriculum in the liberal arts	2	4	4
V. Effort to discourage expansion of course offerings; consolidation of some courses		1	
VI. Process of curricular change itself (too difficult, cumbersome)		1	1
VII. Calendar issue (should it be changed from semester to 4-1-4 basis?)		2	
VIII. Revision of Mathematics Department curriculum		1	
IX. Revision of Physics Department curriculum		1	
X. Revision of Religion and Philosophy Department requirements (required courses for all students)		1	1
XI. Pass-fail grading system: should it be instituted?		1	

Table 16

Curricular Issues Cited--Moravian College

	Cited by		
Issue	Librar-ians	Faculty members	Department chairmen and aca-demic deans
I. Major revision of curriculum and calendar (to 4-1-4 plan)	4	8	5
II. Non-Western Studies (new courses within de-partments)	1	1	
III. Founding of Art Department			1
IV. Master of Arts in Teaching: should such a program be started?		1	
V. Elimination of basic, general courses; encour-agement of too-early spe-cialization		2	
VI. Revision of History Department offerings		1	

Table 17

Curricular Issues Cited--Waynesburg College

| | Cited by | | |
| | Librarians | Faculty members | Department chairmen and academic deans |
Issue			
I. Routine change in departmental offerings	2	5	4
II. Negro History Course	1		
III. Dropping of composition requirement	1	1	
IV. Undue proliferation of courses		1	
V. Development of new Mathematics Program		4	1
VI. Development of Music Education Program		1	
VII. Establishment of Chemistry Department as a separate entity			1
VIII. Should Education and Psychology Departments be separated?			1
IX. Need for data processing equipment to modernize Business Administration courses		1	
X. Social Science requirement in the core curriculum: how large should it be?		1	
XI. Balance of emphasis between pre-professional and liberal arts preparation in the curriculum		1	1

Table 18

Curricular Issues Cited--Geneva College

	Cited by		
Issue	Librar-ians	Faculty members	Department chairmen and aca-demic deans
I. General revision of core curriculum; reduction of Bible requirement; Capstone Course	2	3	3
II. Calendar revision (should college change from the semester plan to 4-1-4 plan, or some other arrangement?)	2		1
III. Problem of scheduling of courses and laboratories to allow certain extracurricular activities	1		
IV. Humanities Course (interdisciplinary course for freshmen and sophomores)		4	4
V. Development of Biochemistry Course by the Biology and Chemistry Departments		2	
VI. Revision of Biology Department courses		1	
VII. Reduction of Social Science requirement in the core curriculum			1
VIII. Revision of Business Administration course offerings		1	

Table 19

Curricular Issues Cited--Ursinus College

Issue	Cited by		
	Librar-ians	Faculty members	Department chairmen and aca-demic deans
I. Ursinus Plan (reduction of core requirements for graduation)	3	1	4
II. Expansion of offerings of particular departments (History, Philosophy, Political Science, Business Administration)		3	1
III. Should Master's Degree Programs be started?		1	1
IV. Setting up of Fine Arts Department		2	1
V. Interdisciplinary Course (Chemistry-Physics-Math) for Science majors	1	1	1
VI. Relevance of English Department offerings (i.e., should the department continue to emphasize the classics, or turn to current issues in literature?)		1	
VII. Should pass-fail grading be instituted?		1	

thus of interest primarily as an indication of important trends in curricular issues at a cross-section of small liberal arts colleges during the past half decade.

More specific questions were asked to determine the respondent's actual role and participation in these curricular issues, his role in curriculum development in general, and, in the case of the non-librarian respondent, his perception of the role of the librarians on his campus in curricular matters. Faculty and administration respondents were also asked for their opinion concerning the role that they felt the college librarians should play, in general, in curriculum development.

Responses to the open-end questions concerning the major curricular issues at the college were coded and quantified with a view to determining any statistically significant differences among the librarians, faculty members, and administrators in regard to knowledge of, and interest in, these issues.[1] Briefly, a respondent would be credited with a "point" for each particular aspect of a curricular issue that he touched upon in the course of the discussion of that issue.

While, obviously, no strong conclusions about the relative de-

Table 20

Average Number of Aspects Discussed of First
Curricular Issue Cited, by Class

Class	Number	Average score
Chief librarians	10	4.6
Reader services librarians	9	3.3
Technical services librarians	12	3.7
Humanities faculty	32	4.8
Social Science faculty	30	4.9
Natural Science faculty	30	4.8
Department chairmen	40	6.3
Academic deans	10	7.5
	173	

Average score, all classes: 5.2

grees of knowledgeability of respondents may be reached on the basis of a few interviews at one college, when one combines the total
number of interviews taken at all colleges (183), some significant
and interesting findings begin to appear.   Table 20 shows the average number of aspects considered of a curricular issue by each
class of respondent.   Most noteworthy here is the fact that all
classes of librarians (chief librarians, technical service librarians,
reader services librarians) fall below all other classes of respondents, although the chief librarians, with an average "score" of 4.6,
come close to the nonadministrative faculty.

This general tendency becomes more apparent when one ex-
amines a compressed frequency distribution (compressed in that all
librarians are grouped together, in one category, all faculty members without administrative responsibilities in another, and the department chairmen and academic deans in another.   The chief fiscal
officers of the colleges studied were not asked the sequence of questions which related to curriculum).   (See Table 21.)

Table 21

Number of Aspects of First Curricular Issue
Discussed--Combined Categories

	0-3	4-5	6-7	8-12	Total
Librarians	13 (42%)	14 (45%)	4 (13%)	0 (0%)	31
Faculty members	23 (25%)	33 (36%)	27 (29%)	9 (10%)	92
Department chairmen and academic deans	1 (2%)	16 (32%)	19 (38%)	14 (28%)	50
TOTAL	37 (21%)	63 (36%)	50 (29%)	23 (13%)	173

$X^2 = 33.68 > 16.81$ (X^2 6 dF @ .01 P)

The scores were combined by defining zero through three as the lowest category, four and five as the second, scores of six and seven as the third, and scores of eight through twelve as the highest. The result is highly significant, statistically. Looking at this table, one can appreciate the meaning of this significance when one sees that 87 percent of the librarians in the survey scored five or under, where 61 percent of faculty members and only 34 percent of department chairmen fell into this category. Also, no librarian scored in the top category, as opposed to 10 percent of faculty members and 28 percent of the department chairmen and academic deans who achieved this level.

Comparison of Particular Aspects of Issue Discussed

It may be useful, at this point, to go beyond an examination of the total scores to look at those aspects of the issue that respondents most frequently discussed, and to see whether or not there are significant differences in the way in which the different classes of respondents dealt with these questions.

Table 22 gives the twelve categories of response utilized to code data obtained in the open-end questions concerning issues, together with the percentage of respondents touching on this aspect of the issue, and whether or not there was a significant proportional difference among the three classes of respondents discussing this aspect. It also indicates whether or not faculty members considered an aspect of the cited issue more frequently than the librarians. Looking at these variables individually, one can see interesting facets which tend to fill out the picture given by the raw total of categories discussed.

Especially noteworthy is the fact that of the twelve coding categories used, application of the chi-square test of proportions showed a statistically significant result in six. That is, there was a relationship between the class of the respondent and whether or not he considered a particular topic. Also noteworthy is the fact that the proportion of faculty members (not including department chairmen) discussing a particular topic was higher than the propor-

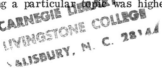

Table 22

Aspects of Curricular Issue One Cited by Respondents

	Aspect of issue cited	Percent of respondents citing	Statistically significant difference in response by class?
1.	Mentions individuals	60	Yes
2.	Mentions committees	69	Yes*
3.	Cites process	65	Yes*
4.	Cites relation to educational philosophy of the college	26	Yes*
5.	Cites impact on students	41	Yes*
6.	Cites impact on faculty	16	No*
7.	Cites impact on library	1	No
8.	Considers issue from college-wide point of view	88	No
9.	Considers issue in relation to teaching effectiveness	19	Yes*
10.	Considers final decision-making power	92	No*
11.	Cites issue as controversial	31	No*
12.	Cites effect on finances of the college	9	No*

*Indicates faculty members had a higher rate of response than librarians.

tion of librarians doing so in nine of the twelve categories. The librarians surpassed the faculty only in regard to categories one, seven, and eight (Mentions Individuals; Impact on the Library; Considers Issue from College-Wide Point of View). In none of these three aspects of the issue was the superiority of the librarians' percentage of response statistically significant. For example, 58 percent of the librarians interviewed mentioned specific individuals involved in the issue they cited, as opposed to 52 percent of faculty members (see Table 23). In category seven, only one librarian out of thirty-one interviewed considered the impact of any curricular issue on the library, a result which must be considered somewhat astonishing in itself. One faculty member out of ninety-two considered this aspect of the issue cited. The third category in which the librarians surpassed the faculty members in percentage of response was in considering the issue they had cited from a college-wide rather than from a departmental point of view. Ninety percent of the librarians interviewed did this, as opposed to 85 percent of the faculty members.

Table 23

Respondents Citing Individuals Involved
In First Curricular Issue

	Individuals not cited		Individuals cited		Total
Librarians	13	(42%)	18	(58%)	31
Faculty members	44	(49%)	48	(52%)	92
Department chairmen and academic deans	13	(26%)	37	(74%)	50
TOTAL	70	(41%)	103	(60%)	173

$X^2 = 6.43 > 5.99$ (X^2 2 dF @ .05 P).

As anticipated, the highest rate of response was obtained in those categories where consideration of an aspect of the issue was

"cued" by questions in the interview schedules; that is, where questions in the interview schedule invited attention to aspects of an issue.   These were category ten (Cites Final Decision-Making Power
in the Issue), cited by 92 percent of respondents; and category eight
(Considering the Issue from a College-Wide Point of View), discussed by 88 percent.   The lowest rate of response was in regard
to category seven (Impact on the Library), already mentioned,
where only 1.2 percent of the respondents (one librarian and one
faculty member) considered the relationship of the issue cited to the
college library.

    Summarizing the findings accumulated in regard to the first
curricular issue cited as "most important," it has been found that,
on a general level, the librarians address themselves to a significantly smaller number of aspects of the curricular issue cited than
do faculty members or department chairmen and deans.   Looking at
individual aspects of the issue cited, faculty members surpassed the
librarians in proportion of response in nine out of the twelve coding
categories used to analyze the data.   These results may be taken
as an indicator of less knowledge of, and interest in, curriculum
development on the part of college librarians.

Involvement of Respondent in Curricular Issue Cited

    How do the above findings coincide with other indicators of
the library's, or librarian's, role in college decision making relating to curriculum?   Each respondent was asked whether he had a
role in regard to the issue he or she had cited, and whether or not
this involvement was typical of his or her usual role.   The distribution of response to this question is shown in Table 24, in which like
responses, or similar responses, are combined.   Statistical testing
indicates a highly significant relationship between class of respondent and type of response.   Especially noteworthy in this table is the
high percentage of librarians responding "no involvement" (42% as
against 9% of faculty members), and the considerably lower proportion of librarians reporting lower, moderate, or peripheral involvement than faculty members (45% as opposed to 70%).   As one might

Table 24

Involvement of Respondent in Curricular Issue Cited

	Closely involved	Involved	Peripheral involvement	No involvement	Total
Librarians	0 (0%)	4 (13%)	14 (45%)	13 (42%)	31
Faculty	4 (4%)	16 (17%)	64 (70%)	8 (9%)	92
Department chairmen and academic deans	14 (28%)	23 (46%)	13 (26%)	0 (0%)	50
TOTAL	18 (10%)	43 (25%)	91 (53%)	21 (12%)	173

$x^2 = 75.91 > 16.81$ (x^2 6 dF @ .01 P).

expect, the department chairmen and deans tended to dominate the response categories indicating greater involvement and influence.

Respondent's Sources of Information
Concerning Curricular Issues

A person's sources of information concerning developments, that is, how he finds out what is going on, are frequently a useful indicator of that individual's status in a community. Operating on this assumption, respondents were asked what their source of information was concerning the curricular issues they had cited. Table 25 shows the distribution of response to this question. Perhaps the most noteworthy point about this distribution is the fact that 53 percent of librarian respondents fell into the lowest response category

Table 25

Respondent's Source of Information Concerning
Curricular Issue Cited

	First-hand information	Intermediate source	Peripheral source	Total
Librarians	5 (17%)	9 (30%)	16 (53%)	30
Faculty members	21 (23%)	42 (46%)	29 (32%)	92
Department chairmen and academic deans	38 (76%)	7 (14%)	5 (10%)	50
TOTAL	64 (37%)	58 (34%)	50 (29%)	172

(reliance upon more formal sources of information), whereas only 32 percent of faculty members were coded here. This finding is perhaps explained by the greater contacts the average faculty member will have with his departmental colleagues, which possibly would

indicate greater isolation on the part of most of the librarians. No
statistical significance may be drawn from this table, however.

Respondent's Perception of His Department's (or the Library's) Role and Influence in Curriculum Development

In order to obtain a reading of the interviewee's perception
of his department's (including the library's) influence and involvement in decision making relating to curriculum, as compared with
the influence of other departments at the college, all faculty (including department chairmen) and librarian respondents were asked
to rate their department's influence, indicating whether its influence
was greater than, equal to, or less than that of other departments.
Table 26 shows the tabulation of response to this question, and application of the chi square test of proportions produces a statistically significant result. Only ten percent of the librarians felt that
the library had as much influence over the development of curriculum as other departments, whereas 63 percent of faculty members

Table 26

Respondent's Perception of His Department's Involvement
and Influence in Curricular Change

	Greater influence	Influence and involvement equal to that of other departments	Less influence than other departments	Total
Librarians	0 (0%)	3 (10%)	28 (90%)	31
Faculty members	21 (23%)	37 (40%)	34 (37%)	92
Department chairmen	8 (20%)	20 (50%)	12 (30%)	40
TOTAL	29 (18%)	60 (37%)	74 (45%)	163

X^2 = 32. 63 > 13. 27 (X^2 4 dF @ .01 P).

and 70 percent of department chairmen felt that their department
had an influence equal to or greater than that of other departments.

Perceptions by Non-Librarians of the College
Librarian's Role in Curriculum Development

In order to obtain an assessment of the librarian's role in
curricular decision making as seen by non-librarians in the sample
(to compare with the librarians' own statements concerning their involvement), faculty members, department chairmen, and academic
deans were asked specifically to describe this role, as they perceived it to be. The results of this questioning were remarkably
similar to the results obtained in questioning the librarians themselves concerning their involvement. Where 87 percent of librarians indicated that they either were not involved at all or only involved in a peripheral way in the development and outcome of the
curricular issue which they had cited, 84 percent of faculty members, department chairmen, and academic deans indicated that they
saw the library and librarians as occupying a passive, supportive
role in regard to curricular decision making. Some typical comments illustrating this point of view are: "They [the librarians]
are agents to get the books faculty and students need," according to
one dean. "He keeps us informed as to the effect of planning on
the library," said one faculty member. Many (52%) went further
and stated that the librarian had no role whatever in curriculum development. This point of view was well expressed by one academic
dean: "totally peripheral." "Almost nil" was the comment of one
faculty member. One other faculty member commented: "He [the
librarian] avoids exercising any influence in curriculum planning."
Table 27 shows this distribution. There is no statistically significant relationship between the class of the respondent and his perception of the role of the librarians.

What the Role of the Library and Librarians
Should Be in Curriculum Development

All classes of respondents were asked what they felt "should
be the role of the library, and the librarians, in regard to the de-

Table 27

Librarian's Role in Curriculum As Seen by Non-Librarians

	High involvement, very active	Same role as faculty member	Supportive role	Little or no role	Total
Humanities faculty	1 (3%)	4 (13%)	7 (22%)	20 (63%)	32
Social Sciences faculty	1 (3%)	4 (13%)	9 (30%)	16 (53%)	30
Natural Sciences faculty	0 (0%)	4 (13%)	9 (30%)	17 (57%)	30
Department chairmen	1 (3%)	4 (10%)	15 (38%)	20 (50%)	40
Academic deans	1 (10%)	3 (30%)	5 (50%)	1 (10%)	10
TOTAL	4 (3%)	19 (13%)	45 (32%)	74 (52%)	142

velopment of the curriculum of the college." Responses were coded
into three categories indicating roughly: (1) active, involved participation in curriculum development; (2) passive, supportive, consult-
ing role; and (3) no role at all. Table 28 shows the distribution of
response to this question. It is interesting to note the very low

Table 28

What the Role of Librarians Should
Be in the Curriculum

	Active, involved role	Sup- portive role	No role at all, or very periph- eral one	Total
Librarians	6 (19%)	22 (71%)	3 (10%)	31
Faculty members	7 (8%)	54 (59%)	31 (34%)	92
Department chairmen and academic deans	3 (6%)	32 (64%)	15 (30%)	50
TOTAL	16 (9%)	108 (62%)	49 (29%)	173

$x^2 = 9.64 > 9.48$ (x^2 4 dF @ .05 P).

proportion, even of librarians, who envisage an active, involved
role for the library in the development of curriculum. Also noteworthy is the fact that one-third (34%) of faculty members and close to
one-third (30%) of department chairmen and academic deans felt that
the library and librarians had no place whatever in curricular decision making.

   Some typical reactions to this question were: "They should
build up the collections and consult concerning courses." "The library should get research materials and materials for teaching. It
is a service department and should not have a role in curriculum."

One faculty member frankly stated: "I can't see a role for librarians in the development of the curriculum." Among librarian respondents, one stated: "The library has a supportive role in regard to curriculum, but should consult more in regard to its development." Another librarian, however, said: "I can't see any role in curriculum change for librarians. We could make suggestions regarding materials but that's all."

While there are differences in perceptions of what the college library's and the college librarians' role should be in the development of the curriculum of the college, it would seem that most respondents foresee only a passive or actually nonexistent role for the library in this area.

Strata Analysis

A secondary goal of this study was to determine whether or not there are significant differences in the relationship of college librarians to decision-making in liberal arts colleges which give relatively strong support to their libraries and in colleges giving relatively poor library support.

To check this, the same tests were run on each stratum of colleges as were applied to the overall data. The results of this testing must be described as negative: no statistically significant differences were found between the performance, or response, of librarians at colleges in the top stratum and librarians at colleges in the lower strata.

In great measure, this result is due to the small number of respondents once the total number is divided into four strata. No statistically significant conclusions are possible even with the same combination of original coding categories used for the overall sample.

Tables 29 through 33 have been compiled from frequency distributions obtained in each stratum for some of the key variables concerning curricular development already used to analyze the total number of respondents at all colleges. In view of the small numbers involved, the most that can be said concerning them is that they are interesting. No clear patterns emerge from the data.

Table 29

Percent of Librarians and Faculty,* by Strata, Scoring Six
or Above in Analysis of First Curricular Issue Cited

	Librarians		Faculty	
Stratum	Number	Percent	Number	Percent
S-1	2	33	6	32
S-2	0	0	15	56
S-3	0	0	11	41
S-4	2	33	4	21

*Does not include department chairmen.

Table 30

Percent of Librarians and Faculty Members* Citing
Involvement and Some Influence in
Curricular Issues Cited

	Librarians		Faculty	
Stratum	Number	Percent	Number	Percent
S-1	2	33	7	37
S-2	1	11	4	15
S-3	0	0	5	19
S-4	1	17	4	21

*Does not include department chairmen.

Table 31

Percent of Faculty Members* and Librarians Citing
Direct or "Inside" Information Source Regarding
Curricular Issues Cited

	Librarians		Faculty	
Stratum	Number	Percent	Number	Percent
S-1	2	33	8	42
S-2	1	11	7	26
S-3	0	0	3	11
S-4	2	33	3	16

*Does not include department chairmen.

Table 32

Number and Percent of Librarians and Faculty Members*
Responding That Their Department Has Influence Over
the Development of Curriculum Equal To or Greater
Than That of Other Departments

	Librarians		Faculty	
Stratum	Number	Percent	Number	Percent
S-1	0	0	11	58
S-2	0	0	17	63
S-3	2	20	18	67
S-4	1	17	12	63

*Does not include department chairmen.

Table 33

Percent of Respondents Indicating That the
Library Should Have an Active, Involved
Role in Curriculum Development

	Librarians		Faculty		Department chairmen and academic deans	
Stratum	Number	Percent	Number	Percent	Number	Percent
S-1	2	33	2	11	0	0
S-2	2	22	3	11	2	13
S-3	2	20	1	4	1	7
S-4	0	0	1	5	0	0

Summary

In terms of overall scores obtained by adding the number of analytical categories a respondent touched on in discussing the questions related to the first curricular issue that he cited, there was a highly significant relationship between the class of the interviewee (librarian, faculty member, or department chairmen or academic

dean) and the number of aspects of an issue that he or she discussed.   This finding would indicate that the librarians interviewed
were less informed and less interested in curricular decision making than were other members of the population.   A breakdown of
the categories used to analyze the data regarding curricular issues
cited tends to support this conclusion.

The results of more direct questioning of respondents concerning the involvement and influence of the library and librarians
in the development of the curriculum of the college tend to coincide
with, and lend credence to, the above conclusions.   These results
present a picture of the librarians as uninvolved both as individuals
and as a department in the issues that they cited; as reliant, generally, upon formal and peripheral sources of information concerning these issues; and as largely uninterested in pursuing a more
active and involved role, a finding that may be somewhat influenced
by the fact that they appear to be operating in an environment which
would deny to the librarian any other than an entirely passive role,
if that, in curriculum development.

No statistically significant differences could be found in the
librarians' relationship to decision-making in curriculum matters at
colleges in the top support stratum as opposed to the other strata
of the sample.

Note

1.   For a detailed explanation of the methodology of coding the re-
     sponses to the open-end questions in the interview schedules,
     see Appendix I.

Chapter IV

THE ROLE OF COLLEGE LIBRARIANS IN BUDGETING

This chapter describes and analyzes the results of those questions in the interview schedules which probed the relationship of the college librarians to the decision-making process in college budgeting. As with the curriculum sequence of questioning, respondents were asked to cite what they considered to be the one or two budgetary issues which they felt had been the most important to come up at the college in the past two or three years. They were then questioned as to who was involved in the issue, who made the final decision on it, etc. More direct questions were then asked concerning the interviewee's own involvement in the issue, his department's perceived influence in budgeting, etc. Data regarding the issue cited were coded through the establishment of categories, or aspects of the issue discussed.

Budgetary Issues Cited

Tables 34 through 43 show the budgetary issues cited at the various campuses and the classes of respondents citing these issues. It will be noted that some of the issues appear to be of a departmental nature rather than of college-wide importance. This is true to a somewhat greater extent than was the case with regard to the curricular issues cited in Chapter III. This point is noted because it may possibly be an indication of the greater isolation of both librarians and faculty members from the decision-making process in budgeting at small liberal arts colleges.

Comparison of Number of Aspects of
First Budgetary Issues Discussed

The first indicator, or test, used in relation to the librarian's role in budgeting is a comparison of the number of aspects of
(cont. p. 76)

65

Table 34

Budgetary Issues Cited--Hamilton College

	Cited by			
Issue	Librarians	Faculty members	Department chairmen and academic dean	Fiscal officer
I. Expansion of the college through opening of coordinate women's college (Kirkland College)	1		1	1
II. Need for new library building (now being planned)	1			
III. Long-range planning to support salary increases for faculty		3	2	
IV. Desire of some faculty for a role in the process of budgetary decision making		1		
V. Need for more research funds		1		
VI. The 4-1-4 Plan: how to support it financially				1

Table 35

Budgetary Issues Cited--Dickinson College

	Cited by			
Issue	Librarians	Faculty members	Department chairmen and academic dean	Fiscal officer
I. Adequate scholarship funds		2		
II. Adequate library budget to build collections	1		2	
III. Faculty salaries: how to keep them competitive			1	
IV. Process of budgeting itself. Feeling on part of some faculty budgeting process has been tightened up too much. Feeling on part of fiscal officer that it hasn't been tightened up enough.		2		1
V. Rivalry for funds between science departments and other departments		1		
VI. Rivalry for funds between academic departments and auxiliary services	1			
VII. Ceiling on number of faculty-- faculty not allowed to grow in size		2	1	
VIII. Expansion plans for library building	1			
IX. General shortage of funds at the college		3	1	

Table 36

Budgetary Issues Cited--Thiel College

	Cited by			
Issue	Librar-ians	Faculty members	Department chairmen and aca-demic dean	Fiscal officer
I. Loss of guaranteed salary for summer school teaching (due to new minimum registration requirement for summer courses)			1	
II. Need for more instructors in the Chemistry Department		1		
III. Need for larger library book budget		3		
IV. New construction program; building priorities	1			
V. Student-faculty ratio too high; too many large sections		1		
VI. General shortage of funds at the college			3	
VII. Need to raise faculty salaries		1	1	1
VIII. Competition for funds between academic departments and service departments		1		
IX. Need to acquire more federal grants	1			

Table 37

Budgetary Issues Cited--Bloomfield College

Issue	Cited by			
	Librar-ians	Faculty members	Department chairmen and aca-demic dean	Fiscal officer
I. New science building; building priorities	1			
II. Purchase of a country club out of the city for eventual con-struction of a new campus		4	2	
III. Need for larger library budget		1		
IV. General lack of funds at the college		2	2	1
V. Obtaining funds for an ex-perimental psy-chology labora-tory		1		

Table 38

Budgetary Issues Cited--Lycoming College

	Cited by			
Issue	Librar-ians	Faculty members	Department chairmen and aca-demic dean	Fiscal officer
I. The Lycoming Plan: how could it be financed? (Lycoming Plan: curricular and calendar change)		6	2	
II. Financing of new academic center (largely paid for out of operating revenues)		2	2	
III. Use of students as teaching assistants			1	
IV. General shortage of funds; critical financial state of the college; instructional budget too high; faculty-student ratio too low				1

Table 39

Budgetary Issues Cited--Elizabethtown College

Issue	Cited by			
	Librarians	Faculty members	Department chairmen and academic dean	Fiscal officer
I. Need for larger library budget	2	2	1	
II. Competition for building space; argument over what departments will be quartered where		1	2	1
III. Need to maintain balance between auxiliary enterprises and instructional program				1
IV. Need for higher faculty salaries		2	1	
V. Process of budgeting; need for more flexibility		1	1	
VI. Reduction of government grants causing tighter budget in some science departments		1		
VII. Favoritism toward science departments in budgeting		1		

Table 40

Budgetary Issues Cited--Moravian College

Issue	Cited by			
	Librar-ians	Faculty members	Department chairmen and aca-demic dean	Fiscal officer
I. Process of budgeting itself; lack of informa-tion on budgeting; business manager not involved enough in making up the budget. Budget being restructured; 10-year projection made up.	2	1	1	
II. Need for larger library budget	2	3	2	
III. New science building; building priorities		2	1	
IV. Need for more scholarship money		1		1
V. Tuition level; need to raise it to meet college's needs versus student's ability to pay				1

Table 41

Budgetary Issues Cited--Waynesburg College

	Cited by			
Issue	Librarians	Faculty members	Department chairmen and academic dean	Fiscal officer
I. Need for more funds for field trips		1		
II. Need for college to obtain data processing equipment and a computer tie-in with a large computing center		1	1	
III. Planning and construction of Humanities building; building priorities			1	1
IV. General shortage of funds; budget restrictions	1	3	2	
V. Need to upgrade the library; more funds needed to build the collections	1			
VI. Need to improve faculty salaries		3	1	
VII. Renovation of the student center				1

Table 42

Budgetary Issues Cited--Geneva College

Issue	Cited by			
	Librar-ians	Faculty members	Department chairmen and aca-demic dean	Fiscal officer
I. Need to up-grade faculty salaries and planning for this	2	3	3	1
II. Implementa-tion of a program of recruitment of students				1
III. Process of budgeting itself; now greatly im-proved over past years			1	
IV. Should the college pay pro-fessional organi-zation dues for faculty members?		1		
V. Need for more funding for speech clinic		1		

Table 43

Budgetary Issues Cited--Ursinus College

| Issue | Cited by | | | |
	Librarians	Faculty members	Department chairmen and academic dean	Fiscal officer
I. Need for and planning of new library building	1	1	1	
II. Building priorities		2		
III. Need for more library book funds		1		
IV. Need for higher faculty salaries			1	
V. Problem of budgeting college funds to match funds provided by government grants				1
VI. Issue of capital debt budgeting				1
VII. Process of budgeting itself	1	1	1	

the budgetary issue cited as "most important" which the interviewee considered. As was the case with the curricular issues analyzed, this measure is seen as an indicator of relative degrees of knowledgeability and interest in budgetary decision making on the part of respondents.

Combining scores as well as classes of respondent yields the distribution shown in Table 44. While no statistical significance may be drawn from this distribution, there are a number of quite important points worth noting. Most interesting are the comparative totals of librarians and faculty members. Whereas 16 percent of librarians scored five or above, 24 percent of faculty members achieved this level. This difference is not nearly as clear cut as

Table 44

Number of Aspects Discussed, First Budgetary
Issue (Combined Categories)

	0-2	3-4	5-6	7-11	Total
Librarians	13 (42%)	13 (42%)	4 (13%)	1 (3%)	31
Faculty members	35 (38%)	35 (38%)	20 (22%)	2 (2%)	92
Department chairmen and academic deans	9 (18%)	13 (26%)	19 (38%)	9 (18%)	50
Fiscal officers	0 (0%)	2 (20%)	2 (20%)	6 (60%)	10
TOTAL	57 (31%)	63 (34%)	45 (25%)	18 (10%)	183

in regard to the first curricular issue (see Table 21) where 39 percent of the faculty members fell in the upper two categories as opposed to only 13 percent of the librarians. The upper ranges of the distribution are occupied largely by interviewees with some administrative responsibility, the department chairmen, academic deans, and fiscal officers.

Because of the large number of individuals who did not cite
a second budgetary issue, no analysis of the responses of those
who did would be meaningful, and none is attempted.

Comparison of Particular Aspects of
First Budgetary Issue Discussed

As with the first curricular issue cited, however, it may be
of value to look behind the total number of aspects of an issue discussed to examine the particular aspects themselves.   Table 45
shows the analytical categories used, together with the percentage
of interviewees touching on this aspect of the issue, and whether or
not a statistically significant relationship was found between consideration of this aspect and class of interviewee.   Also indicated
is whether or not faculty respondents were proportionately more
likely to discuss this point than the librarians.   (For a detailed explanation of the method used to code the open ended questions relating to curriculum, budgeting, and staffing, see the appendix.)

One of the more noteworthy features of this table is the fact
that a statistically significant difference in response between classes
of interviewee is obtainable (through application of the chi-square
test of proportions) in seven out of the ten coding categories.   However, in some cases, when one looks further at the data and compares the performance of the librarians with that of the faculty members, as in category one (Mentioning Specific Individuals), one finds
that the significant statistic computed is due largely to the especially
strong tendency of respondents with administrative duties (department chairmen, deans, and fiscal officers) to consider this aspect
of the issue.   That is, the difference in proportion of librarians and
the proportion of faculty members mentioning specific individuals involved in the issue they have cited is relatively small.   Table 46,
which shows the distribution of respondents citing individuals, re-
veals that 58 percent of librarians and 48 percent of faculty members did this, whereas 80 percent of the department chairmen and
deans and 100 percent (all ten) of the fiscal officers mentioned specific individuals.   The same is true of category four (Considers Relationship of the Issue to the Instructional Program of the College),

Table 45

Particular Aspects of Budgetary Issue One
Cited by Respondents

	Aspect cited	Percent citing	Statistically significant difference in response by class?
1.	Mentions individuals	61	Yes
2.	Mentions committees	20	Yes*
3.	Cites process	31	Yes
4.	Considers issue in relation to the instructional program of the college	18	Yes*
5.	Gives opinions as to adequacy of budget in terms of size, speed of processing, etc.	40	No
6.	Cites impact of issue on the students	6	No*
7.	Cites impact of issue on the faculty	24	Yes*
8.	Considers issue from a college-wide rather than departmental view	63	Yes*
9.	Considers final decision-making authority	69	Yes*
10.	Cites issue as controversial	15	No*

*Indicates faculty members had a higher rate of response than librarians.

Table 46

Number of Respondents Citing Particular Individuals
Involved in Issue Cited

	Individuals not mentioned		Cited individuals		Total
Librarians	13	(42%)	18	(58%)	31
Faculty members	48	(52%)	44	(48%)	92
Department chairmen and academic deans	10	(20%)	40	(80%)	50
Fiscal officers	0	(0%)	10	(100%)	10
TOTAL	71	(39%)	112	(61%)	183

$X^2 = 20.84 > 11.34$ (X^2 3 dF @ .01 P).

Table 47

Number of Respondents Citing the Relationship of the Issue
Cited to the Instructional Program of the College

	Not cited		Cited		Total
Librarians	28	(90%)	3	(10%)	31
Faculty members	82	(89%)	10	(11%)	92
Department chairmen and academic deans	35	(70%)	15	(30%)	50
Fiscal officers	5	(50%)	5	(50%)	10
TOTAL	150	(82%)	33	(18%)	183

$X^2 = 16.41 > 11.34$ (X^2 3 dF @ .01 P).

where only 10 percent of librarians and 11 percent of faculty members considered this aspect of the issue. On the other hand, 30 percent of department chairmen and deans and half of the fiscal officers did so (see Table 47). Apparently, the major dichotomy in knowledge of, and interest in, budgeting issues is between the librarians and faculty members on the one hand, and the chairmen, deans, and fiscal officers on the other.

The librarians surpassed, proportionately, the faculty members in three areas: categories one (Mentions Individuals), three (Cites Process Followed in this Issue), and five (Gives Opinions as to the Adequacy of the Budget, etc.). In category one, it has already been seen that much of the strength of the statistic computed is due to the strong showing of administrators. The same is true of category three (Process), where 26 percent of librarians and 16 percent of faculty members described the process whereby the budgetary issue they cited was handled. But 50 percent of the department chairmen and deans and 90 percent of the fiscal officers did this. Table 48 gives the distribution of response in this category.

The third category in which the librarians surpassed the faculty members (category five, Gives Opinions Concerning Adequacy of the Budget, etc.) is illustrative of another feature of this type of coding. Since this category would contain any comment ranging from a complaint about the size of the budget allotted for some relatively minor departmental matter to a sophisticated statement of the needs of the college, it would tend to act as a leveling agent in coding. This hypothesis is borne out by the insignificant result of statistical testing, indicating little relationship between class of interviewee and response to this category. Table 49 shows the complete distribution of those who commented in this manner.

In general, a consideration of the individual coding categories for budgetary issues reinforces the conclusions derived from the comparison of the overall count of aspects discussed. These are that faculty members tend to be somewhat better informed than the librarians, achieving a higher percentage of response in seven out of the ten categories. However, the major differentiation in the

Table 48

Number of Respondents Citing the Process of Budgeting
in Relation to the Issue Cited

	Does not cite process		Cites process		Total
Librarians	23	(74%)	8	(26%)	31
Faculty members	77	(84%)	15	(16%)	92
Department chairmen and academic deans	25	(50%)	25	(50%)	50
Fiscal officers	1	(10%)	9	(90%)	10
TOTAL	126	(69%)	57	(31%)	183

$X^2 = 34.30 > 11.34$ (X^2 3 dF @ .01 P).

Table 49

Number of Respondents Expressing an Opinion
Concerning the Adequacy of the Budget

	Does not express an opinion		Expresses an opinion		Total
Librarians	18	(58%)	13	(42%)	31
Faculty members	62	(67%)	30	(33%)	92
Department chairmen and academic deans	26	(52%)	24	(48%)	50
Fiscal officers	4	(40%)	6	(60%)	10
TOTAL	110	(60%)	73	(40%)	183

population appears between interviewees with administrative responsibilities and those without them.

Involvement of Respondent in Budgetary Issue Cited

As with the analysis of the librarians' relationship to the development of curriculum at the college, more direct questions were
asked to relate the respondent specifically to budgetary decision
making both on a college-wide level and in his department. All
three general categories of interviewees were questioned as to their
involvement in the budgetary issue they had cited and further probed
as to whether or not this involvement and influence was typical of
their usual role in budgeting at the college.   Table 50 gives a frequency distribution of the responses.

Most noteworthy in this table is the dichotomy which appears
very strongly between those who are involved on a college-wide basis and those who are not.   One hundred and seventeen interviewees
(64%), most of them librarians and faculty members, indicated that
they were totally uninvolved in budgeting outside their departments.
While 68 percent of librarians interviewed are among those citing
no involvement, as opposed to 95 percent of faculty members, the
lower percentage of librarians is due almost entirely to the chief
librarians.   These people have a tie to the administrative hierarchy,
which apparently makes the decisions in budgeting, through their
negotiation of the library budget.   While no statistical significance
may be drawn from this distribution, it is obvious that the dichotomy between those involved and those not involved is very marked.
Essentially, only those interviewees with some sort of administrative role cite involvement.

Comparison of Involvement of Librarians and Faculty Members in Development of their Departmental Budget

Primarily as a means of achieving a further comparison between the involvement in budgetary decision making of librarians
and of faculty members, both these groups of respondents were
questioned concerning the process of budgeting within their depart-
(cont. p. 86)

Table 50

Involvement in Budgeting in the College

	Highly involved		Moderately involved		Peripheral, or only slight involvement		Not involved at all		Total
Librarians	0	(0%)	8	(26%)	2	(7%)	21	(68%)	31
Faculty members	0	(0%)	2	(2%)	3	(3%)	87	(95%)	92
Department chairmen and academic deans	10	(20%)	31	(62%)	0	(0%)	9	(18%)	50
Fiscal officers	10	(100%)	0	(0%)	0	(0%)	0	(0%)	10
TOTAL	20	(11%)	41	(22%)	5	(3%)	117	(64%)	183

Table 51

Involvement in Budgeting in the Department or the Library

	Highly involved; initiating role		Involved		Only slightly involved		No involvement		Total
Chief librarians	10	(100%)	0	(0%)	0	(0%)	0	(0%)	10
Reader services librarians	0	(0%)	0	(0%)	4	(44%)	5	(56%)	9
Technical services librarians	1	(8%)	1	(8%)	5	(42%)	5	(42%)	12
Humanities faculty	0	(0%)	6	(19%)	18	(56%)	8	(25%)	32
Social Sciences faculty	1	(3%)	2	(7%)	22	(73%)	5	(17%)	30
Natural Sciences faculty	1	(3%)	7	(24%)	18	(60%)	4	(13%)	30
Department chairmen	35	(88%)	2	(5%)	3	(8%)	0	(0%)	40
TOTAL	48	(30%)	18	(11%)	70	(43%)	27	(17%)	163

Table 52

Involvement in Budgeting in the Department or the Library, Combined Categories

	Highly involved; initiating role	Involved	Only slightly involved	No involvement	Total
Librarians	11 (36%)	1 (3%)	9 (29%)	10 (32%)	31
Faculty members	2 (2%)	15 (16%)	58 (63%)	17 (19%)	92
Department chairmen	35 (88%)	2 (5%)	3 (8%)	0 (0%)	40
TOTAL	48 (30%)	18 (11%)	70 (43%)	27 (17%)	163

$X^2 = 107.93 > 16.81$ (X^2 6 dF @ .01 P).

Note: Discrepancies in percentage totals due to rounding.

ment (or the library) and their involvement in this process. Table
51 shows the responses to the questioning. A most interesting feature of this table is the indication of a relatively greater degree of
participation in departmental decision making regarding budgeting
on the part of faculty members as opposed to librarians. Fifty-six
percent (five out of nine) of the reader services librarians and 42
percent of technical services librarians (five out of 12) indicated
that they had nothing to do with the makeup of the library budget.
This contrasts with the following percentages for faculty members
other than department chairmen: 25 percent of faculty members in
the Humanities; 17 percent of those in the Social Sciences; and 13
percent of natural scientists indicated no involvement in departmental budgeting. Also worth noting in regard to library and departmental budgeting is the fact that, as might be expected, all ten
of the chief librarians interviewed stated that they were responsible
for making up the library budget.

       The relatively greater degree of participation in budgeting in
faculty departments by non-chairmen is made more obvious by the
results of combining both class (row) and response (column) categories, as is done in Table 52. Despite the fact that all chief librarians (as shown by the previous table) were coded with the department chairmen, 32 percent of all librarians interviewed stated
that they were uninvolved in the development of the library budget.
This is compared to only 19 percent of faculty members who gave
the same response. Another significant figure in this regard is
that while 16 percent of faculty members (aside from department
chairmen) cited a substantial degree of participation in budget decision making (most of these people stated that the whole department
got together and developed the budget), only three percent of librarians could be coded in this category. While 63 percent of faculty
members were coded in the fourth category, the librarians' proportion is significantly lower in this category only because the chief librarians were coded with the department chairmen in Column 1.
Statistical testing shows a significant relationship between class of
interviewee and response to this series of questions. Even allowing

for the fact that responses of the department chairmen caused a
part of this result, it is apparent that a significant difference exists
between librarians and faculty members in the extent to which they
participate in development of the budget.

Respondents' Sources of Information Concerning Budgetary Issue Cited

As with curricular issues, respondents were queried as to
their sources of information regarding budgetary issues.   No sur-
prises were found in responses to these questions, and the resulting
frequency tables are not reproduced.   Suffice to say that, with very
few exceptions, only department chairmen and chief librarians cited
top administrators as sources of budgetary information; that prac-
tically no one received budgetary information from a faculty com-
mittee--perhaps a further indication of the centralized nature of
budgetary decision making in small liberal arts colleges; and that
the prime source of budgetary information for most librarians and
faculty members was the chief librarian or the department chairman, with such miscellaneous sources as faculty meetings, formal
reports, and the "grapevine" being a close second.

Perceived Influence of the Library in Budgeting

In order to probe the perceptions of all interviewees regarding the influence of the library in college budgeting, use was made
of a technique in which respondents were asked to place the library
as a department on a scale of ten, comparing it to other academic
departments.

Respondents were first asked what they considered to be the
most influential academic department in the college in regard to
budgeting.   Table 53 shows the interesting response to this question.
Listed are all the departments which were cited at least five times
as being "most influential" in budgeting, and also the number of
times respondents refused to pick a department.

Interviewees were then asked to cite the department which
they considered to be the one that was least influential in regard to
budgeting at the college.   Table 54 shows the response to this
(cont. p. 91)

Table 53

Most Influential Department in Budgeting

	0*	B	BA	C	E	FA	H	Ph	PE	Phy	S	Total
Librarians	7 (23%)	0 (0%)	1 (3%)	6 (20%)	1 (3%)	1 (3%)	3 (10%)	0 (0%)	1 (3%)	3 (10%)	6 (20%)	29
Faculty members	17 (19%)	6 (7%)	4 (4%)	16 (17%)	2 (2%)	2 (2%)	2 (2%)	2 (2%)	2 (2%)	8 (9%)	25 (27%)	86
Department chairmen and academic deans	8 (16%)	5 (10%)	2 (4%)	13 (26%)	2 (4%)	3 (6%)	0 (0%)	2 (4%)	2 (4%)	2 (4%)	8 (16%)	47
Fiscal officers	3 (30%)	0 (0%)	1 (10%)	2 (20%)	0 (0%)	0 (0%)	0 (0%)	1 (10%)	0 (0%)	0 (0%)	3 (30%)	10
TOTAL	35 (19%)	11 (6%)	8 (4%)	37 (20%)	5 (3%)	6 (3%)	5 (3%)	5 (3%)	5 (3%)	13 (7%)	42 (23%)	172

*0 = no department cited; B = Biology; BA = Business Administration; C = Chemistry; E = English; FA = Fine Arts; Ph = History; Ph = Philosophy; PE = Physical Education; Phy = Physics; S = Sciences.

Note: Only those departments which were cited five times or more are included in this table.

Table 54

Least Influential Department in Budgeting

	0*	BA	Cl	E	FA	FL	M	Ph	PE	Phy	R	So	Total
Librarians	16 (52%)	1 (3%)	2 (7%)	0 (0%)	0 (0%)	2 (7%)	2 (7%)	1 (3%)	2 (7%)	1 (3%)	0 (0%)	2 (7%)	29
Faculty members	28 (31%)	2 (2%)	3 (3%)	5 (6%)	6 (7%)	6 (7%)	6 (7%)	5 (6%)	9 (10%)	3 (3%)	5 (6%)	5 (6%)	83
Department chairmen & academic deans	16 (32%)	1 (2%)	4 (8%)	1 (2%)	2 (4%)	4 (8%)	2 (4%)	2 (4%)	4 (8%)	0 (0%)	6 (12%)	4 (8%)	46
Fiscal officers	3 (30%)	1 (10%)	1 (10%)	0 (0%)	0 (0%)	1 (10%)	1 (10%)	0 (0%)	2 (20%)	1 (10%)	0 (0%)	0 (0%)	10
TOTAL	63 (35%)	5 (3%)	10 (6%)	6 (3%)	8 (4%)	13 (7%)	11 (6%)	8 (4%)	17 (9%)	5 (3%)	11 (6%)	11 (6%)	168

*0 = no department cited; BA = Business Administration; Cl = Classics; E = English; FA = Fine Arts; FL = Foreign Languages; M = Mathematics; Ph = Philosophy; PE = Physical Education; Phy = Physics; R = Religion; So = Sociology.

Note: Only those departments which were cited five times or more are included in this table.

Table 55

The Library's Perceived Influence in Budgeting, Ranked on a Scale of Ten

	0	1	2	3	4	5	6	7	8	9	10	Total
Librarians	3 (10%)	2 (7%)	1 (3%)	1 (3%)	2 (7%)	5 (17%)	6 (20%)	3 (10%)	2 (7%)	4 (13%)	1 (3%)	30
Faculty members	4 (4%)	2 (2%)	2 (2%)	6 (7%)	4 (4%)	11 (12%)	15 (16%)	20 (22%)	18 (20%)	6 (7%)	4 (4%)	92
Department chairmen and academic deans	3 (6%)	0 (0%)	0 (0%)	5 (10%)	2 (4%)	2 (4%)	6 (12%)	9 (18%)	14 (28%)	6 (12%)	3 (6%)	50
Fiscal officers	0 (0%)	1 (10%)	0 (0%)	0 (0%)	1 (10%)	0 (0%)	0 (0%)	3 (30%)	3 (30%)	1 (10%)	1 (10%)	10
TOTAL	10 (6%)	5 (3%)	3 (2%)	12 (7%)	9 (5%)	18 (10%)	27 (15%)	35 (19%)	37 (20%)	17 (9%)	9 (5%)	182

Note: 0 = low, or no ranking; 10 = high.

query. Possibly noteworthy here is the large percentage of librarians (52%) who could not or would not commit themselves on this
question.

Having thus established perceived extremes of influence over
budgeting on the part of departments, respondents were then shown
a scale of ten numbers (drawn in the form of a ladder with ten at
the top and zero at the bottom) and asked to place the library on
this scale. Table 55 shows the somewhat incongruous response to
this question. The word incongruous is used because of the fact
that 69 percent of interviewees saw the library as being in the top
half of all departments in budgetary influence. Five percent of respondents even removed their previous top choice and placed the library there. Furthermore, this ranking holds true in all classes
of respondent. There are no significant differences in the rankings
of the library by the various classes. This result would appear to
fly in the face of the other findings reported in this chapter, which
have tended to indicate that the librarians had very little to do with
budgeting outside their own department (or within, in many cases).

A possible explanation of this incongruity is that respondents
often interpreted this question as meaning "how does the library
rank in regard to the question as to who gets most?" Since libraries are extremely expensive departments to operate, the answer to
this interpretation of the question is quite obvious: the library
ranks high in budgetary influence. Further support for this explanation of the library's high standing may be seen in Table 53, which
shows the departments cited as most influential. Fifty-six percent
(a highly significant percentage when one notes that no non-science
department achieved more than 3% of the "vote") of respondents
stated that either "the sciences" as a group, or a science department such as chemistry or physics, were (or was) at the top of the
ladder. The reason for this ranking is fairly obvious, and in line
with the reason for the library's ranking. Science departments re-
quire expensive appropriations for equipment and laboratory materials; ergo, these departments are "most influential." (It might be
noted parenthetically that the breakdown of faculty member response

to this question was as follows: of faculty members in the Humanities, 66 percent cited the sciences as being at the top; 53 percent
of the Social Sciences faculty and 60 percent of the Natural Sciences people themselves placed the sciences or one of their departments at the top of the list.)

Respondents' Satisfaction with the Budgeting Process in their Departments

One further measure relating to the role of the librarian in
college budgeting is deserving of mention. In order to obtain in-
sight into the degree of satisfaction of respondents of all classes
with budgetary decision-making processes, they were asked whether
or not they would like to see a change in the process by which
their department's (or the library's) budget is developed and ap-
proved. Table 56 shows that there is no significant difference between the various classes of respondents and their desire to change

Table 56

Should the Process of Budgeting Be Changed?

	No change desired		Change desired		Total
Librarians	20	(67%)	10	(33%)	30
Faculty members	66	(72%)	26	(28%)	92
Department chairmen and academic deans	41	(82%)	9	(18%)	50
Fiscal officers	6	(60%)	4	(40%)	10
TOTAL	133	(73%)	49	(27%)	182

the process. Particularly noteworthy is the fact that two-thirds or
more of both librarians and faculty members (67% and 72%, re-
spectively) desired no change in the process of developing their department's budget. The percentage of staff librarians expressing
satisfaction with the process is even higher than this figure, as
half of the ten chief librarians interviewed did express a desire for

some change. It would appear, then, that both faculty members and staff librarians were reasonably satisfied with the apparently largely authoritarian pattern of budgetary decision making in the colleges studied.

Comparison of Response by Sample Strata

As was the case with the questions relating to the librarians' role in curriculum development, it was found that once the colleges were divided by strata, the number of cases was too small and the responses too scattered to allow for statistically significant testing of differences in response among the various classes of respondents. It is possible to compare the percentages of librarians and faculty members responding to questions in certain ways, but, due to the small number of cases involved, it is not possible to have a meaningful test of significance of these differences.

Table 57 shows the percentages of librarians, faculty members, and department chairmen and deans in each strata who discussed five or more of the different categories used for analysis relating to the budgetary issue that they had cited. It is interesting to note that the librarians' percentage fluctuates from 50 percent in the top strata to zero percent in the second, while the other two classes remained relatively constant.

Table 58 gives the percentage of librarians and the percentage of faculty members who responded that they were not at all involved in college-wide budgeting, in each stratum. In interpreting this table, it must be remembered that the faculty member category does not include the department chairmen; the librarians category does include the chief librarians, who would of necessity have some sort of tie to the budgeting authorities of the college by virtue of their administrative status. Were they to be placed in a separate category, the staff librarians would be 100 percent noninvolved.

One last table (Table 59) gives a picture of the relative degrees of involvement of librarians and faculty members in the making up of their departmental budget.

Table 57

Percentage of Respondents Citing Five or More Aspects
of the Budgetary Issue Discussed, by Strata

Strata	Librarians		Faculty members		Department chairmen and academic deans	
	Percent	Number	Percent	Number	Percent	Number
S-1	50	3	26	5	60	6
S-2	0	0	26	7	60	9
S-3	10	1	26	7	53	8
S-4	17	1	16	3	50	5

Table 58

Percentage of Librarians and Faculty Members Stating That
They Were Not Involved in the Budgeting
Issue Cited, By Strata

Strata	Librarians		Faculty members	
	Percent	Number	Percent	Number
S-1	67	4	95	18
S-2	67	6	100	27
S-3	70	7	93	25
S-4	67	4	90	17

Table 59

Percent of Librarians and Faculty Members Citing
Noninvolvement in Departmental Budgeting,
by Strata

	Librarians		Faculty members	
Strata	Percent	Number	Percent	Number
S-1	33	2	37	7
S-2	44	4	15	4
S-3	30	3	11	3
S-4	17	1	16	3

Summary

This chapter has been devoted to a study of the role of the
college librarians in budgetary decision making in the colleges making up the sample. It was found that there was a significant relationship between the knowledge of and interest in budgeting issues
at the college and the class of respondent. However, there was
far less difference between librarians and faculty members than
was the case with regard to curricular issues. In addition, a
larger number of respondents cited no budgetary issue than was the
case with curricular issues. Analysis of the categories utilized to
code the material relating to the issues cited by respondents backed
up, generally, these findings, as would be expected.

Direct questioning of respondents concerning their role in
college-wide budgeting matters revealed a strong dichotomy, or contrast, between those involved and those who were not. These latter
consisted largely of staff librarians and faculty members other than
department chairmen. There was no significant difference between
the response of these two groups.

Regarding budget processing within the department or library,
however, it was evident that some faculty departments, at least,
have a considerably more democratic process of developing the
budget than is the case in the library. A significantly higher num-

ber of faculty members reported involvement at this level than did
librarians.

Testing the perceived influence of the library, as a department, in the budgetary decision-making process at the college
proved inconclusive due to an apparently widespread tendency on the
part of respondents to consider this matter in terms of "who gets
most?" rather than "who has most influence?"

Questioning regarding need for change in budgeting procedures revealed little sentiment in favor of change. The overwhelm-
ing majority of staff librarians and faculty members other than department chairmen are evidently quite content with little or no role
in the budgetary process.

No statistically significant differences were found in regard
to the above variables considered on the basis of sample strata.

Chapter V

THE ROLE OF COLLEGE LIBRARIANS IN
KEY APPOINTMENTS

The third area of important decision making in small liberal
arts colleges to be considered in this study is that of appointments.
This chapter is devoted to the presentation and analysis of the data
accumulated in this area.

Key Appointments Cited

As with curricular and budgetary issues, respondents were
asked to cite what they felt had been the most important appointment at the college "in the past couple of years." Respondents
were not restricted to any particular type of appointment, and as a
result, except where a very outstanding appointment had taken place
(viz. the appointment of an Academic Dean at Elizabethtown College), there was a considerable degree of "scatter" in their choices.
Tables 60 through 69 give the appointments cited as "most important" at each college.

Comparison of Number of Aspects
Discussed of Appointment Cited

Interviewees were then asked what people and departments
were involved in making the appointment, who or what group made
the final decision, etc. The information obtained in these open-end
questions was coded by applying a series of response categories to
the material given by the interviewees. The number of analytical
categories to which a respondent spoke was totaled in order to obtain an indicator of this person's knowledge of, and interest in, appointments at the college. Table 70, which compresses both row
and column variables, shows a statistically significant difference between the class of the respondent and the number of aspects of an
appointment discussed. However, it is apparent that the differences
(cont. p. 103)

Table 60

Key Appointments Cited--Hamilton College

	Cited by		
Appointment	Librarians	Faculty members	Department chairmen and academic dean
I. New President (1968)	3	7	4
II. New Biology Department Chairman		1	
III. Director of Long-Range Planning			1
IV. Vice President for Development & Resources			1

Table 61

Key Appointments Cited--Dickinson College

	Cited by		
Appointment	Librarians	Faculty members	Department chairmen and academic dean
I. New Head Librarian			1
II. New Academic Dean	3	9	3
III. Chemistry Department Chairman			1
IV. New Associate Dean		1	

Table 62

Key Appointments Cited--Thiel College

Appointment	Cited by		
	Librar-ians	Faculty members	Department chairmen and aca-demic dean
I. Department chairmen in general		4	3
II. Head Librarian	2	1	
III. Music Department Chairman	1	1	1
IV. New Dean of Men		1	
V. Chairman of Education Department		3	1

Table 63

Key Appointments Cited--Bloomfield College

Appointment	Cited by		
	Librar-ians	Faculty members	Department chairmen and aca-demic dean
I. Department chairmen in general		1	
II. Chemistry Depart-ment Chairman			1
III. Nursing Department Chairman			1
IV. Head Librarian		2	2
V. Vice President and Treasurer	1		
VI. Coordinator of Cooperative Education Program	1	1	
VII. Process of search-ing for new President and new Academic Dean	1	3	

Table 64

Key Appointments Cited--Lycoming College

	Cited by		
Appointment	Librar-ians	Faculty members	Department chairmen and aca-demic dean
I. English Department Chairman	1		
II. Sociology Depart-ment Chairman		1	
III. Physics Department Chairman	1		1
IV. Appointment of Act-ing President, 1968-1969	1	6	
V. Process being used to search for new Presi-dent		2	2
VI. Appointment of former Academic Dean			2

Table 65

Key Appointments Cited--Elizabethtown College

	Cited by		
Appointment	Librar-ians	Faculty members	Department chairmen and aca-demic dean
I. Academic Dean	2	5	7
II. Education Depart-ment Chairman	1		

Table 66

Key Appointments Cited--Moravian College

		Cited by	
Appointment	Librar-ians	Faculty members	Department chairmen and aca-demic dean
I. Process of appoint-ment of department chairmen in general	1		1
II. New President (appointed spring 1969)	3	7	2
III. Admissions Director			2
IV. Academic Dean		1	
V. Religion Department Chairman		1	
VI. Art Department Chairman			1

Table 67

Key Appointments Cited--Waynesburg College

		Cited by	
Appointment	Librar-ians	Faculty members	Department chairmen and aca-demic dean
I. Process of appoint-ing department chairmen in general	2	6	2
II. Chemistry Depart-ment Chairman		1	1
III. Language Depart-ment Chairman	1		2
IV. Chairmen of newly divided Psychology and Education Departments	1	1	1

Table 68

Key Appointments Cited--Geneva College

| | | Cited by | |
	Librar-ians	Faculty members	Department chairmen and aca-demic dean
Appointment			
I. Chairman of Physics Department		1	
II. Head Librarian		1	2
III. New Business Manager	3	7	3

Table 69

Key Appointments Cited--Ursinus College

| | | Cited by | |
	Librar-ians	Faculty members	Department chairmen and aca-demic dean
Appointment			
I. Appointment of department chairmen in general		1	1
II. Assistant Director of the Evening School		1	
III. Process of appointment of new administrative officers in general			1
IV. Administrative Assistant to the President (later made Vice President for Administration)	1	4	3
V. Appointment of Academic Dean to additional office of Vice President for Academic Affairs		2	
VI. New Business Manager	1		
VII. Process to be used to find and select a new President		1	1

Table 70

Number of Aspects Discussed of Appointment Cited

	0-2		3-4		5-11		Total
Librarians	14	(45%)	12	(39%)	5	(16%)	31
Faculty members	31	(34%)	45	(49%)	16	(17%)	92
Department chairmen and academic deans	7	(14%)	26	(52%)	17	(34%)	50
TOTAL	52	(30%)	83	(48%)	38	(22%)	173

$X^2 = 12.44 > 9.48$ (X^2 4 dF @ .05 P).

are somewhat less striking than was the case in regard to the curricular issues.

Examining Table 70, it is apparent that the proportion of librarians in the lowest category (zero to two aspects of the appointment touched on) is higher (45%) than that of faculty members (34%), and lower in the middle category (three to four categories discussed; librarians 39%; faculty members 49%). The difference in the top category is insignificant. The lesser degree of differentiation between the classes of respondents, together with the low range of the scores, would appear to make the study of appointments a somewhat less useful indicator of perceived status in decision making at colleges of the type studied in this investigation. (The range in number of aspects discussed of the appointment cited was zero to seven; the range for the first curricular issue cited was zero to eleven; and for the first budgetary issue, zero to nine.) It would appear on the basis of these tables, and the appointments cited, at least, that few individuals aside from the academic deans and department chairmen are very knowledgeable concerning appointments outside their immediate area. In any event, differences in response between the classes (librarians, faculty members, department chairmen and deans), while present, are less visible and less significant than was the case in the two other areas.

Comparison of Particular Aspects Discussed of the Appointment Cited

Table 71 shows the results of analysis of the specific categories used to code the information obtained in the open-end questions on key issues cited. Especially noteworthy is the fact that
application of the chi-square test of proportions to each of these
categories revealed a significant difference in response between the
various classes of respondents in only one case, that of citing individuals involved in whatever appointment was cited. Also significant is the fact that of the eleven categories, only three [(1) Cites
individuals; (6) Comments concerning process of appointment; and
(7) Cites final decision-making power] were considered by a majority of the respondents. Also, two categories were never cited
[(8) Cites ability of department head to veto appointments in his own
department, and (11) Cites appointment as controversial].

In five of the nine categories that respondents touched on,
the faculty members scored higher than the librarians, but in none
of these cases was the difference in proportions statistically significant. The librarians cited individuals involved in the appointment
chosen more frequently than did faculty members, and while a significant statistic can be computed for the distribution of results in
this category (see Table 72), the difference between the proportion
of librarians and proportion of faculty is minor (52% of librarians
and 48% of faculty members mentioned individuals involved). It is
obvious that most of the strength of the statistic computed comes
from the much higher proportion of department chairmen and academic deans (74%) who cited individuals involved.

Also noteworthy in Table 71 is the fact that of the three other analytical categories where the librarians surpassed faculty members [(4) Cites student involvement in appointment, (5) Cites librarian involvement, and (7) Cites final decision-making authority], no
statistically significant difference was found between the proportions.
And, of the three, category four (student involvement) was considered only by six percent of respondents, and category five (librar-

Table 71

Aspects of Key Appointment Discussed by Respondents

	Aspect cited	Percent citing	Statistically significant difference?
1.	Cites individuals	56	Yes
2.	Cites committee involved	34	No*
3.	Cites faculty involvement in the appointment	50	No*
4.	Cites student involvement in the appointment	6	No
5.	Cites librarian involvement in the appointment	1	No
6.	Comments concerning procedure involved in making this appointment	72	No*
7.	Cites final decision-making authority in this appointment	82	No
8.	Cites ability of department head (library or academic) to veto any appointment to his own department	Not cited	
9.	Cites influence of the appointment on the curriculum and educational philosophy of the college	4	No*
10.	Cites the influence of the appointment on the administrative functioning of the college	10	No*
11.	Cites the appointment as being controversial	Not cited	

*Indicates faculty members discussed this aspect more frequently than librarians.

Table 72

Respondents Citing Individuals Involved
in Appointment Cited

	Does not cite individuals	Cites individuals	Total
Librarians	15 (48%)	16 (52%)	31
Faculty members	48 (52%)	44 (48%)	92
Department chairmen and academic deans	13 (26%)	37 (74%)	50
TOTAL	76 (44%)	97 (56%)	173

ian involvement) was considered only by two librarians (1% of all respondents), a fact which in itself may be of some significance.

All in all, from looking at the individual analytical categories, it is not surprising that the results in regard to the total scores are rather inconclusive, particularly when compared to those achieved in the areas of curricular and budgetary issues. These results tend to add strength to the hypothesis already advanced, that both faculty members (aside from department chairmen) and librarians have little to do with appointments not directly related to their own department.

Respondents' Sources of Information Concerning Appointment Cited

This conclusion is strongly reinforced by the results of more direct questioning of respondents concerning their involvement in the appointments cited. Taking the matter of where the individual received information concerning the appointment that he cited, Table 73 shows a strong correlation between class of interviewee and type of response. (Table 73 gives compressed categories both for class [row] variables and response [column] variables.) Only 13 percent of librarians and 11 percent of faculty members cited a "high"

Table 73

Respondents' Sources of Information Concerning Appointment Cited

	First-hand information	Intermediate source	Peripheral source, formal communications, etc.	Total
Librarians	4 (13%)	7 (23%)	20 (65%)	31
Faculty members	10 (11%)	34 (37%)	48 (52%)	92
Department chairmen and academic deans	23 (47%)	13 (27%)	13 (27%)	49
TOTAL	37 (22%)	54 (31%)	79 (46%)	172

Table 74

Involvement of Respondent in Appointment Cited

	Highly involved	Somewhat involved	No particular appointment cited	Not involved	Total
Librarians	0 (0%)	2 (7%)	1 (3%)	28 (90%)	31
Faculty members	1 (1%)	9 (10%)	6 (7%)	76 (83%)	92
Department chairmen and academic deans	11 (22%)	8 (16%)	2 (4%)	28 (57%)	49
TOTAL	12 (7%)	19 (11%)	9 (5%)	132 (77%)	172

source of information (basically, someone intimately involved with
the appointment), while 47 percent of department chairmen and
deans reported such a source. Sixty-five percent of librarians and
52 percent of faculty members cited formal and peripheral sources
of information, as opposed to only 27 percent of department chairmen and deans. While no statistically significant results may be
derived from the distribution, the proportion of the different classes
responding in the different categories makes very clear the dichotomy between those "on the inside" (persons with some administrative responsibility) and those who are not (librarians and faculty
members).

Involvement of Respondent in Appointment Cited
        This dichotomy is made even more explicit by Table 74,
which shows the response to the question of the interviewee's own
involvement in the appointment. (This table is also compressed
both as to row and column variables.) Out of 172 people who answered this question, 132 indicated that they were totally uninvolved
in the appointment that they cited. Ninety percent of librarians interviewed were in this category, 83 percent of faculty members
other than department chairmen, and 57 percent of department
chairmen and deans. While no statistical significance may be derived from this table, these percentages alone are enough to add
strength to the conclusion that neither librarians nor the average
faculty member have much to do with important appointments at liberal arts colleges.

The Role of Librarians in Key Appointments
as Perceived by Faculty Members and Administrators
        With regard to the librarians alone, the hypothesis that in-
terviewees without administrative responsibility are uninvolved in
key appointments is strengthened further by the response to the
question posed to faculty members, department chairmen, and administrators concerning their perception of the role of the librarian.
Asked to characterize the role and involvement of the college librarian in major college appointments, 82 percent of faculty members

Table 75

Role of Chief Librarian in Major College Appointments

	Highly involved	Has same role as other faculty	Little or no involvement	Total
Faculty members	2 (2%)	15 (16%)	75 (82%)	92
Department chairmen and academic deans	1 (2%)	10 (20%)	39 (78%)	50
Fiscal officers	0 (0%)	1 (33%)	2 (67%)	3
TOTAL	3 (2%)	26 (18%)	116 (80%)	145

and 78 percent of department chairmen and deans indicated that the librarian had little or no role. Only two percent of these classes of respondents saw the librarian on their campus as being actively involved in key appointments. See Table 75 for a graphic description of these results.

Comparison of Appointment Process in the Library and Other Academic Departments

It may be useful at this time to look at what data are available concerning the relative degrees of involvement in appointments within the library and other academic departments of librarians and faculty members, as was done in regard to the development of departmental budgets. All classes of respondents were asked a sequence of questions concerning the process of appointment in their department or, in the case of administrators, the library, and any involvement they had in this process.

Table 76 shows a rather interesting result. While all ten chief librarians indicated that they were involved in the staffing of professional positions, eight out of nine (89%) of reader services librarians and seven out of twelve technical services librarians (58%) indicated that they were not. This compares with 53 percent of Humanities faculty and 43 percent of both Social Sciences and Natural Sciences faculty who indicated that they were uninvolved. This difference becomes a bit more apparent in Table 77, where classes of respondents are compressed to four. While 53 percent of all faculty members who are not chairmen indicate involvement, as opposed to 52 percent of librarians, it must be remembered that the proportion of staff librarians is actually much lower because ten of the sixteen librarians citing involvement in staffing in the library are chief librarians. The proportion of staff librarians indicating participation is actually only 19 percent.

Respondent Perceptions of Who Makes the Final Decision in Appointments

Another interesting comparison of professional participation in staffing in libraries and other academic departments is demon-

Table 76

Involvement of Respondents in Staffing in
the Department or Library

	Not involved		Involved		Total
Chief librarians	0	(0%)	10	(100%)	10
Reader services librarians	8	(89%)	1	(11%)	9
Technical services librarians	7	(58%)	5	(42%)	12
Humanities faculty	17	(53%)	15	(47%)	32
Social sciences faculty	13	(43%)	17	(57%)	30
Natural sciences faculty	13	(43%)	17	(57%)	30
Department chairmen	1	(3%)	39	(98%)	40
Academic deans	3	(30%)	7	(70%)	10
Fiscal officers	10	(100%)	0	(0%)	10
TOTAL	72	(39%)	111	(61%)	183

Table 77

Involvement in Staffing in the Department
or Library, Combined Classes

	Not involved		Involved		Total
Librarians	15	(48%)	16	(52%)	31
Faculty members	43	(47%)	49	(53%)	92
Department chairmen and academic deans	4	(8%)	46	(92%)	50
Fiscal officers	10	(100%)	0	(0%)	10
TOTAL	72	(39%)	111	(61%)	183

$X^2 = 39.17 > 11.34$ (X^2 3 dF @ .01 P).

strated by Table 78, which relates to the question of who staff librarians and faculty members feel makes the real decision as to who is appointed. Thirty percent of faculty respondents indicated that the decision was made by the whole department as a group, whereas only three percent of the librarians could say this. On the other hand, 74 percent of librarians indicated that the decision was made by the head librarian while only 33 percent of faculty responded that, essentially, the department chairman made the decision as to who was hired and who was not. Of course, 15 percent of faculty interviewees did indicate that the real decision was made by the academic dean or the president, but if one combines those who stated that either the department chairman or some higher authority makes the decision, one comes up with a total percentage of 48 percent, far below the librarians' 74 percent. It would appear that chief librarians have a much greater degree of control over who works on the professional staff of the library than department chairmen do over who teaches in their departments. As a corollary of this statement, it seems that in a substantial number of cases, faculty departments act as a group in hiring. Only one librarian out of the thirty-one interviewed felt that this was the case in the library

Respondents' Satisfaction with the Appointment Process in their Departments

One further point has possible importance. When respondents were asked whether or not the process of making appointments in their department (or in the library) should be changed, 74 percent of librarians and 74 percent of faculty members saw no need for change. Evidently a fair proportion of both librarians and faculty members are content with not having much of a role in selecting their colleagues. Table 79 shows this graphically.

Comparison of Response by Sample Strata

As with the analysis of the librarian's relationship to the decision-making process in curricular development and budgeting, the number of cases is too small to allow for statistically significant

Table 78

Who Makes Final Decision on Appointments ?

	Department chairman or head librarian	Higher Administrative Official, (President or Academic Dean)	Whole depart- ment	"Other"	Total
Librarians	23 (74%)	0 (0%)	1 (3%)	7 (23%)	31
Faculty members	30 (33%)	13 (15%)	28 (30%)	21 (22%)	92
Department chairmen and academic deans	17 (34%)	11 (22%)	12 (24%)	10 (20%)	50
Fiscal officers	2 (20%)	0 (0%)	0 (0%)	8 (80%)	10
TOTAL	72 (39%)	24 (14%)	41 (22%)	46 (25%)	183

Table 79

Should the Process of Making Departmental
Appointments Be Changed?

	No change needed		Change process		Total
Librarians	23	(74%)	8	(26%)	31
Faculty members	68	(74%)	24	(26%)	92
Department chairmen and academic deans	43	(86%)	7	(14%)	50
Fiscal officers	10	(100%)	0	(0%)	10
TOTAL	144	(79%)	39	(21%)	183

findings once the colleges are divided by strata. However, the
same tables and statistical tests were developed and applied for
each stratum as for the total number of cases. A few of these statistics are interesting and provide indications of possible significance in the data. Tables 80 and 81 show a comparison of librarians (including chief librarians) and faculty members (not including
department chairmen) in two respects: the proportion of both groups
discussing five or more aspects of the key appointments cited; and
the proportion of both groups indicating that they were uninvolved
in the appointments they had cited.

Table 82 compares the percentage of faculty members indicating involvement in staffing in the department with the percentage of
librarians doing likewise. Possibly noteworthy here is the high degree of involvement indicated by respondents at top stratum colleges.

Table 83 shows relative degrees of democratic decision making in regard to appointments in the library and other academic departments. Again noteworthy is the quite high degree of involvement
of all members of a faculty department in choosing their colleagues
at the top stratum schools. The library shows no such progression
from bottom to top strata.

Table 80

Percent of Respondents Discussing Five or More Aspects
of Key Appointments Cited, by Strata

Strata	Librarians		Faculty members	
	Percent	Number	Percent	Number
S-1	33	2	37	7
S-2	0	0	7	2
S-3	20	2	19	5
S-4	17	1	11	2

Table 81

Percent of Respondents Indicating They Were Uninvolved
in Appointment Cited, by Strata

Strata	Librarians		Faculty members	
	Percent	Number	Percent	Number
S-1	83	5	95	18
S-2	100	9	89	24
S-3	100	10	63	17
S-4	67	4	90	17

Table 82

Percent of Respondents Indicating Involvement
in Staffing in Their Department

Strata	Librarians		Faculty members	
	Percent	Number	Percent	Number
S-1	67	4	84	16
S-2	56	5	52	14
S-3	30	3	41	11
S-4	67	4	42	8

Table 83

Percent of Librarian and Faculty Respondents
Reporting Whole Department Makes
Decision on Appointments

Strata	Librarians		Faculty members	
	Percent	Number	Percent	Number
S-1	0	0	68	13
S-2	0	0	37	10
S-3	0	0	15	4
S-4	17	1	5	1

117

Summary

It has been found that librarians are somewhat less informed, interested, and articulate than faculty members concerning key appointments at the colleges studied. However, the differences between the responses of the librarians and the other classes of respondents are not nearly as strong and clear cut as they were in regard to the curricular and budgetary issues cited in Chapters III and IV. Responses in this open-end sequence and responses given in direct questioning of interviewees concerning their sources of information on appointments and their personal involvement in the appointments cited, tend strongly to suggest the same sort of dichotomy between uninvolved librarians and faculty members and involved deans and department chairmen which appeared in regard to the process of budgetary decision making.

Comparing the relative degree of involvement within the library and other academic departments of librarians and faculty members, it was found that faculty members were somewhat more likely to be involved in the appointment process than were all librarians, and considerably more likely to be involved than were staff librarians. Faculty departments were also more likely than the libraries to utilize more democratic methods of decision making in regard to appointments; the choice of professional staff for the library is apparently almost always in the hands of the chief librarian.

Questioning concerning whether or not a change in the process of making appointments would be desirable or not indicated that most respondents were satisfied with the process as it was.

No statistically significant differences were apparent among types of response in regard to the several sample strata.

Chapter VI

SUMMARY, IMPLICATIONS OF THE FINDINGS, AND SUGGESTIONS FOR FURTHER RESEARCH

The primary purpose of this study has been to provide a description of the relationship of college librarians to key areas of decision making in small liberal arts colleges. In addition, some attention has been given to certain miscellaneous variables which bear upon the librarian's relationship, in general, to college society.

First, of the librarians interviewed, most held a professional library degree from an accredited library school, but a majority had a rather short length of service (under seven years) at the colleges they served. They tended to be older people (the majority being over fifty), most were women (although men held eight out of the ten chief librarian's positions), and most were married.

The vast majority of librarians interviewed stated that they had faculty status. However, when one went further and probed for information concerning perquisites and privileges usually associated with full faculty status, a mixed picture appeared. All librarians interviewed were eligible for the faculty retirement plan, and the majority were eligible for service on faculty committees, could vote at faculty meetings, and had faculty titles. On the other hand, none had a faculty contract, few had to meet faculty requirements for appointment, and few could say that they had salaries equivalent to those of faculty members.

Questioning concerning the librarians' role in the committee structure of the college showed the librarians occupying a distinctly peripheral position. Only a minority served on committees at all, and in only two instances were the assignments to committees considered as important or influential in the college community.

Other questions revealed the librarians to be somewhat iso-

119

lated from the college community, at least as perceived by the majority of faculty members and administrators interviewed. The majority, also, of librarians and faculty members saw their closest
contact in the library (faculty members for librarians) only once a
month or less. The most important reason, by far, for faculty-librarian contact was collection building (i.e., book ordering, etc.)

The degree of congruence between the librarians' perceptions
of their role, their feelings as to how other members of the academic community perceived their role, and how faculty members
and administrators actually saw this role provided interesting findings, although none that were statistically significant. The sampling of librarians interviewed in this study showed a tendency on
the part of some librarians to assume that they were seen as either
a separate group on campus or as a part of the administrative
structure of the college, whereas the actual views of the non-librarians tended to line up more closely with the librarians' own concep-
tion of their role. That is, faculty members and administrators
saw the librarians as faculty members about as often, proportionately, as the librarians did themselves.

Turning to the main interest of this study, the relationship
of the librarians to specific key areas of decision making, the peripheral status of college librarians in the academic community, in
most cases, was confirmed.

First, it was found in analysis of the responses to the open-
end questions relating to the curricular issue, or issues, which the
respondent stated was (were) the most important to have come up
at the college in recent years, that there was significant difference
between the number of aspects of these issues discussed by librarians and the number discussed by faculty members and administrators. This result indicates a relative lack of interest and knowledge concerning curricular change among librarians.

More directly related to actual role in curricular decision
making were the answers to direct questioning concerning respondents' involvement in the issues they had cited as being most important. Here there was a highly significant difference between the

responses of the librarians and those of the other classes of respondents. Librarians were far more likely to cite noninvolvement in the issue than were faculty members and administrators.

Answers concerning the respondents' sources of information about curricular issues again indicated lack of involvement on the part of the librarians, but were inconclusive statistically. The same can be said concerning interviewees' perceptions of the influence of their department in curriculum development.

More conclusive evidence relating to the librarians' role in curriculum was obtained by querying non-librarians concerning their perception of the librarians' involvement in curricular decision making. The vast majority (84%) of faculty members and administrators saw the librarians as having little or no role in this area.

While there were differences, as between librarians and other respondents, in the number of aspects discussed of a budgetary issue cited as the "most important" to arise at the college in recent years, and these differences were indicative of less knowledge of and interest in college-wide budgetary issues on the part of librarians than other respondents, this result was somewhat less conclusive than in regard to curriculum development.

Direct questioning of respondents concerning their involvement in the budgetary issue cited showed an apparent strong correlation between class of interviewee and involvement, a correlation, however, which is not susceptible to statistical testing. However, there was apparently very little difference in this area between the involvement of the librarians and the faculty members (other than department chairmen). More significant here than the differences in response among librarians and all other categories was the difference between those interviewees with some administrative responsibility (fiscal officers, deans, department chairmen) and those without such responsibility.

Questioning of respondents concerning the process of budgeting in the library or in their department, and their involvement in this process, showed a highly significant difference between librarians and faculty members. As a generality, faculty were considerably more involved.

Investigation of the role of the librarians in key appointments showed a significant difference between the number of aspects of an appointment cited as being the "most important" at the college in recent years by librarians and the number discussed by other classes of respondents. However, the differences between the librarians and faculty members and administrators were less clear-cut than in the case of curricular issues. Sources of information on the key appointment cited showed a strong dichotomy between those with administrative responsibility and those without. Responses to the question relating to the interviewee's own involvement in the key appointment cited show that faculty members (other than department chairmen), as well as librarians, exhibit a high degree of noninvolvement. While non-librarians saw the librarians as almost totally non-involved in major college appointments, it is significant that faculty members were almost equally uninvolved in key appointments.

As with budgeting, comparison of the involvement of college librarians and faculty members in staffing in their own departments, proved significant. Faculty members showed a far higher degree of involvement than did staff librarians. Also, faculty departments were much more likely than the libraries studied to utilize democratic decision making in the appointments process.

In sum, the librarians do appear overall to have a very minimal role in the mainstream of events at the college; but, in certain areas, they are apparently no more uninvolved than the bulk of the faculty.

Implications of the Findings and
Suggestions for Further Research

There are essentially three general areas of librarianship for which the findings of this study hold implications. First, considering librarianship as a profession, the practitioners at many of the colleges studied seem to have made little progress toward the ideals of more effective integration into the educational program of the college, as stressed over the years by such writers as Branscomb and Knapp. Nor, apparently, have they made much progress

toward the goal of achieving genuine professional status (whether independent professional status as librarians, or as faculty members)
as hypothesized by Bundy and Wasserman.[1] Rather, it would appear that Bidwell's observation that, in many cases, the librarian's
role becomes largely that of a "clerk whose work centers on rou-
tines of book ordering, organizing, and locating within a frame set
for him by the college curriculum" has considerable validity for
many of the libraries visited.[2] To place Bidwell's comment in con-
text, he was hypothetically contrasting the role of the librarian as
"mediator" in subject department rivalries at more selective colleges, or a role as subject specialist at the same type of institution, as opposed to the above-mentioned clerical role. The librarians' apparent lack of involvement in curricular decision making
would seem to make clear their distance from achieving any sort
of professional status as faculty members.

One further implication of the findings of this study for library professionalism relates to the status of the staff librarians.
It would appear, if the college libraries studied are at all repre-
sentative, that college librarians work in a somewhat more bureaucratic and authoritarian environment than do their faculty colleagues.
While one may argue that the greater diversity of the functions of
a library (compared to those of a faculty department) necessitates a
somewhat different organization, it may nevertheless be asked, as
do Bundy and Wasserman,[3] whether or not the hierarchical and
bureaucratic nature of much of library administration may be ham-
pering the development of a more professional service. It is fairly
apparent, at least from the data accumulated in this study, that titles and other academic perquisites are not achieving this end, and
that other such superficial remedies are likely to be as unsuccess-
ful.

A second question posed by the findings of this study relates
to library service itself. The apparent isolation of the library and
librarians from the mainstream of events at the college, coupled
with the equivalent isolation (in some areas) of faculty members,
might lead one to reemphasize the ideal of the centralized library,

mediating between the conflicting demands of the academic departments; or to a reemphasis of the ambitious ideal of integrating the
library with the curriculum to the degree attempted at Monteith College, or as hypothesized in the library-college literature. Possibly
a more realistic response, however, to the evidence of provincial-
ism on the part of librarians and faculty members would be that
Mohammed should "go to the mountain." That is, that rather than
attempt to fight the growing departmentalization of the liberal arts
colleges, librarians would do well to consider modifying their devo-
tion to centralized service and to offer more departmentalized service. It may be argued that departmentalization of library service
may be fine for large universities but impractical for small liberal
arts colleges of the size studied in this investigation, and to an extent this objection has merit. Too great fragmentation of already
inadequate library resources would be a retrogressive step. However, a certain amount of decentralization, of accommodation to the
departmentalization of higher education, would appear to offer the
possibility of improved information service to faculty and students,
and also the possibility of somewhat greater contact with the curriculum and with these other segments of the academic community.
As Daniel P. Bergen has suggested: "To attempt to counter the
centrifugal thrust of the faculty, and the units in which the profes-
soriate works, is unrealistic policy."[4]

     Promotion of more direct, more accessible information serv-
ice through some degree of departmentalization of college library
service relates strongly to the question of library education. A degree of subject specialization would appear to be necessitated by a
program of working closely with faculty and students in departmental information centers. This possibility would be in line with Bidwell's prediction that subject specialization would be an increasingly
strong trend in the "elite" liberal arts colleges in response to the
increasing fragmentation of fields of knowledge.[5] Bergen implies
that teaching would be a desirable activity for librarians who wished
to promote integration with the faculty.[6] All of this further implies
a need for education for academic librarianship beyond the bache-
lor's degree and the professional master's.

Beyond an apparent need for increased subject expertise, the question is raised as to what sort of professional education would be desirable for librarians who intend to operate in liberal arts colleges. Since a certain degree of versatility is necessary in a small professional staff, particularly if one is going to set up one or more subject area libraries, there is much to be said for the typical general core program now in existence at most library schools.[7] However, the general picture obtained from this study, of the library's being outside the mainstream of events at the college, may lead one to suspect that more could be done to prepare librarians for an active role in librarianship in higher education than is the case at present. A course in the sociology of higher education could well be a desirable option for master's candidates planning on entering academic library work. Such an option, or requirement, would be in line with the stress placed upon understanding the community in courses related to public librarianship. And the fact that the librarians' most frequent contact with faculty was related to collection building would also suggest that expanded subject bibliography offerings, where presently not in existence, could help the prospective college librarian prepare for a more professional role.

While demonstrating and deploring the largely passive role of librarians in decision making on small liberal arts campuses, one should perhaps point out that breaking out of this bureaucratic, semi-clerical mold and obtaining entrée to the collegial structure of the faculty is not an easy task, as witnessed by the difficulties encountered by the Monteith College Library project. Here, the amply supported project staff encountered a "pervasive, perhaps largely unconconscious, attitude of rejection on the part of the 'ideal-typical' instructor"[8] in their attempt to attain an active integration of the library into the curriculum of this experimental college of Wayne State University. Nor should one assume that the "ideal-type" college librarian should be one who drops his traditional functions of acquiring, organizing, and disseminating information to rush headlong into academic politics. Obviously the question of the involvement of the librarians in decision making is one of degree.

However, without some effort to break out of the vicious
circle of passive library service and low faculty and administration
expectations of the library, so evident in some of the colleges
studied, the library will remain a peripheral agency in the institution it is set up to serve.   College librarians must make the effort
to become more involved in decision making, whether through committees, where much of the faculty collegial structure resides, or
through more active information services, such as SDI for faculty
departments, or through merely what Bergen called "facultyman-
ship."   Whatever the means chosen (and hopefully all of these and
others would be undertaken), there must first be a recognition on
the part of college librarians that involvement in key areas of decision making is important (or even that it is possible), a recognition which is apparently lacking to a great extent in the colleges
studied.   For without a role in the decision making processes of
the college (the core of any organization, according to Simon[9]) one
can well question whether the institutions these libraries serve are
receiving adequate information service.   Can there be active and
thorough information service when librarians reveal themselves to
be as little interested in the development of the curriculum as they
have in this study?   Can there be adequate service when the librarians are revealed to have little or no involvement, and such little
interest in being involved, in decision making relating to budgeting
and staffing?   One can also question whether or not adequate library and information service can be given if communication is not
a vital and continuing process between the librarians and other members of the academic community rather than being confined largely
to formal requests for services from the collegially organized faculty to the largely bureaucratic and clerical librarians.   In short,
can information and library service be superior, or even adequate,
without involvement?

Suggestions for Further Research:

There are a number of possible areas for further research
relating to the librarians' role in college decision making.   For ex-

ample, one area in which further research might be fruitful is that of information service patterns. Colleges which have adopted a degree of decentralized information service could be studied to determine whether or not this type of service pattern has reduced the isolation of the library to an appreciable degree.

Further inquiry would also seem warranted into the assumption made above that a more democratic administrative style on the part of chief librarians would promote a more professional involvement of the staff librarians both within the library and in the affairs of the college. Is this the case in libraries which have moved toward a more collegial arrangement of responsibility?

And, in regard to the educational qualifications hypothesized as useful for prospective college librarians, follow-up could be done on graduates of library schools which already have a "track" program attempting to give some specialized training to students who have opted for work in a particular type of library. Does this type of specialization, such as it is, give them an advantage in adjusting to the problems of providing active information service in liberal arts colleges?

These are but a few of the questions which could be asked in relation to the implications raised by the data accumulated in this study.

Notes

1. Mary Lee Bundy and Paul Wasserman, "Professionalism Reconsidered," College and Research Libraries, XXIX (January, 1968), 5-26.

2. Charles E. Bidwell, "Librarian, Administrator, and Professor: Implications of Changing College Social Structures," in Libraries and the College Climate of Learning, ed. by Daniel P. Bergen and E.D. Duryea (Syracuse: Syracuse University Press, 1964), p. 67.

3. Bundy and Wasserman, op. cit., p. 14-19.

4. Bergen, op. cit., p. 469.

5. Bidwell, op. cit., p. 66-67.

6. Bergen, op. cit., p. 469.

7. Some empirical evidence for this supposition may be found in James Liesener's dissertation. Liesener found that while some of the "core" areas of librarianship emphasized by the schools are apparently irrelevant to the work of many librarians in large university libraries, these same areas were more useful to librarians working in subject, or special clientele, libraries. James Will Liesener, "An Empirical Test of the Validity of the Core Concept in the Preparation of University Librarians" (unpublished Ph. D. dissertation, University of Michigan, 1967).

8. Knapp, Patricia B. The Monteith College Library Experiment. New York: Scarecrow Press, 1966, p. 31.

9. Simon, Herbert A. Administrative Behavior. 2d ed. New York: The Free Press, 1957.

Appendix

METHODOLOGY

Sample of Colleges

As stated in Chapter I, this study was carried out at private, liberal arts, four-year undergraduate colleges in the states of New York, New Jersey, and Pennsylvania. It was confined to colleges having an enrollment of between eight hundred and two thousand matriculated students, no more than four percent of whom were enrolled in graduate study. Because of some interest, in the planning stages of this investigation, in determining the personal and professional contacts of the members of the academic community, it was decided to eliminate from the population colleges which were staffed in their administrative and faculty positions to a substantial degree by members of a formal religious order.[1]

It was determined, through use of Library Statistics of Colleges and Universities; 1965-1966: Institutional Data,[2] and the Education Directory, 1966-1967, Part 3, "Higher Education,"[3] that thirty-one colleges in New York, New Jersey, and Pennsylvania fitted the above criteria.

In order to obtain more complete and more up-to-date statistical information, a questionnaire was developed and mailed to the chief librarians of these thirty-one colleges. This questionnaire also asked for information on the professional background of the chief librarian and the number of professional librarians and clerks employed in the libraries of these colleges. Sixty-eight percent of the colleges (twenty-one of them) responded to the initial mailing. A telephone call to the chief librarians brought in eight more returns. Only two chief librarians refused to participate in the study at this stage, and their schools were dropped from the population.

As has been mentioned in Chapter I, the annual expenditure,

Table 84

Stratification of College Population

	Annual expenditure, per student, on the library, 5-year average, 1963-64 to 1967-68
Stratum I	
Swarthmore	$206
Vassar	185
Hamilton	139
Dickinson	112
Skidmore	101
Washington & Jefferson	97
Colgate	95
Stratum II	
Bloomfield	86
St. John Fisher	79
Thiel	77
Gettysburg	74
Muhlenburg	74
King's	70
Allegheny	69
Lycoming	69
Stratum III	
Upsala	65
Hartwick	64
Susquehanna	64
Elizabethtown	61
Moravian	61
St. Lawrence	61
Hobart	60
Waynesburg	60
Stratum IV	
Houghton	57
Albright	52
Geneva	47
Lebanon Valley	46
Ursinus	38
Grove City	17

per student, on the library, averaged over the five year period 1963 to 1968 was chosen as the variable with which to rank and stratify the population.   Table 84 shows the resulting ranking and stratification.   The tie between Hobart and Waynesburg prevented the creation of three equal strata of seven colleges each and one of eight.   Two colleges, were chosen through use of a random number table, from the top stratum of seven, three each from the two middle strata of eight, and two from the bottom stratum of six.

Of the colleges chosen, two refused to participate in the study at this juncture.   Significantly, perhaps, both colleges were in the bottom stratum and both vetoes came from the presidents of the institutions.   Replacements were selected from this stratum, again through the use of a random number table.

Data Collection Instruments

The use of personal interviews for the collection of data for this study was decided on for several reasons: first, it was felt that much more data could be obtained in the course of several interviews of thirty to forty-five minutes than could be obtained from even a very detailed questionnaire.   Secondly, it was assumed that the response would be better, and more complete, to attempts to interview personally than to an attempt to obtain data from an extensive questionnaire.   That is, it was recognized that a low return is frequently a problem in using questionnaires, with the percentage of responses tending to drop in relation to the length and detail of the questionnaire.   Thirdly, the greater flexibility of the interview, the ability to probe where an unclear response is received or to clarify a question when a respondent does not understand questions, was felt to be a vital consideration. [4] Another consideration in the decision to rely upon interviews was the somewhat more intangible benefits that it was hoped could be obtained from actually visiting the college to be studied.   That is, a factor of observation was added to the data collection process which, it was felt, would add to a general understanding on the part of the investigator of the type of college chosen as the population for this study.

An interview schedule of one hundred and seven items was compiled and pretested at two colleges taken from the population. [5] A complete sequence of interviews was taken at each college, following the procedures planned for the study. As a result of this experience, the single interview schedule was discarded and replaced with three separate schedules (with many overlapping questions, however) for the three types of respondents: librarians, faculty members, and administrators.

Essentially, each of these interview schedules consisted of five sections: first, basic classificational and biographical data (rank, tenure, length of service at the college, etc.; and, for the librarians, their status as members or non-members of the faculty); secondly, exploration of decision making at the college in regard to the curriculum, and the respondent's relationship to it; third, budgetary decision making and the respondent's involvement therein; fourth, key appointments at the college and the respondent's involvement, if any, in them; and fifth, general questions relating to the respondent's perceived status in the college and his perception of the status of others (particularly the librarians).

The second, third, and fourth sections, relating to curricular, budgetary, and staffing decision making, were almost entirely composed of open-ended questions. Respondents were asked what they considered to have been the most important issues to have developed at the college in the past two or three years, [6] and then queried as to who and what was involved in these issues, where they obtained information concerning the issue, who made the final decision in its solution; and, in the case of the non-librarians, whether any of the library staff were involved.

The goal of all phases of the interview schedule was to develop a picture of the role of the librarians of the college in relation to important decision making at the college, both as seen by themselves and by others.

Sampling of Faculty Respondents

Because of the size of the faculty population, and the desirability of achieving a cross section of opinion from this group, a stratified random sample was again resorted to. Stratification was carried out by dividing the faculty into the three disciplinary sub-divisions of the Humanities, the Social Sciences, and the Natural Sciences, with the members of the various teaching departments being assigned to a stratum as described in Chapter One. Three faculty members were chosen from each stratum through use of a random number table, with a fourth being chosen from the Humanities stratum (the largest stratum at all ten of the colleges) if the faculty numbered more than ninety. A separate, stratified random sample of four department chairmen was also taken at each college, two being chosen from the Humanities departments, and one each from the Social Sciences and Natural Sciences.

Data Collection

The interviewing for this study was conducted during the spring of 1969. Generally, three and one-half days were sufficient to complete the eighteen or nineteen interviews at each college. However, in two cases, four and one-half days were required.

In any study utilizing sampling of a population, the rate of response (return of questionnaires, rate of agreement to be interviewed) is significant. In the case of this study, the willingness of respondents to be interviewed was at most times encouraging. The rate of refusal to be interviewed was extremely low among faculty members. Of the faculty contacted for interviews, only 14% either could not be reached or refused to be interviewed. They were replaced with alternates.

Regarding the other respondents in the study, there was no case in which an administrator or a librarian either refused to be interviewed or could not be reached.

Data Analysis

A major task in the analysis of the data accumulated in this study has been the construction of a coding manual with which information obtained in the personal interviews could be tabulated,

analyzed, and to the largest degree possible, manipulated statistically for significant correlations. Concerning the open-end questions, categories for coding must, in effect, be created from the
information supplied by the interviewees in response to the questions posed to them. Backstrom and Hursh recommend taking a
25 percent sample of all interview schedules, writing down all the
answers to a particular open-ended question, and then establishing
meaningful categories for these questions for coding purposes.[7]
This was the procedure followed for a substantial number of the
open-end questions in this investigation.

Because certain questions were not only open ended, but also
of the type where the interviewee was allowed, to a great extent,
to pick his own type of response, a further refinement of this
method of analyzing open-ended questions was necessary. In relation to the sequences of open-end questions covering the particular
key issues chosen by respondents (that is, those regarding decision
making in curriculum, budgeting, and staffing), a series of general
categories was developed to describe several aspects of the particular issue covered by each respondent. Table 85 shows the descrip-
tive categories utilized in the coding manual to analyze the information supplied in answer to the open-end questions relating to curricular decision making.

These categories of response were applied to specific questions in the interview schedules, with all writing in the space allotted for these questions being read for applicability to these categories. In coding these sections of the interview schedule, a
"one" code was given for each category of response to which the
interviewee addressed himself, and a "zero" code for each category
to which he did not. The number of "one" codes has been totaled
to give a rough indicator of the respondent's knowledge of, and interest in, the issues or appointments which he cited as being of
top importance. While it may be objected that this type of scoring
gives a premium to the most articulate respondents, this point is
answered to some extent by the fact that an interviewee would be
coded "one" only once for discussing, for example, specific indi-

Table 85

Coding Categories Used for Curricular Issues Cited

Respondent mentions specific people involved in the development of the issue

1. Yes   0. No

Mentions specific committees involved in the development of this issue

1. Yes   0. No

Describes the process of curricular change in this particular instance

1. Yes   0. No

Describes the relationship of this curricular issue to the educational philosophy of the college

1. Yes   0. No

Speaks of, or considers, the impact of the change on the students

1. Yes   0. No

Considers the impact of the change on the faculty

1. Yes   0. No

Considers the impact of the change, or issue, on the library

1. Yes   0. No

Considers the issue from a college-wide point of view, as opposed to a purely departmental point of view

1. Yes   0. No

Considers the issue from the point of view of teaching effectiveness

1. Yes   0. No

Considers the final decision-making power in this issue

1. Yes   0. No

Cites issue as controversial

1. Yes   0. No

Considers the effect of the particular curricular issue on the finances of the college

1. Yes   0. No

viduals involved in the issue which he cited, no matter how loqua-
cious he became on the subject.

Another objection that may be posed to this method of coding open-ended questions, and which should be borne in mind in interpreting the results, is that a respondent will be coded "one" for
even a passing reference to an aspect of the issue he cited while
the same code will be given to a respondent who, for example, describes the process of curricular change in the issue chosen in
some detail.   There is in this method of coding, therefore, a built-
in tendency to diminish real differences of knowledge regarding key
decision-making issues.

Another built-in bias in this type of analysis, at least as
regards the interview schedules used in this study, is that certain
categories used in the analysis relate to specific questions asked
in the interview, whereas others do not.   For example, all interviewees were asked specifically to cite the person or persons who
made the final decision on the issue under discussion.   Therefore,
all respondents would be coded "one" for this category except those
who answered that they "didn't know" or those who had cited no issue at all.   On the other hand, no question was asked requesting
the interviewee to consider the impact of the issue cited upon the
faculty or the library.   The effect of this factor in the categorization of responses to this type of open-end question is to almost
guarantee a certain minimum score to all respondents and to tend
to make real differences in knowledgeability between respondents
less apparent.

Nevertheless, it is felt that, despite these limitations, such
categorization and scoring of open-ended questions of this type is
worth the time required to carry it out, and that it does provide a
useful, albeit crude, indicator of a respondent's knowledge of and
interest in the key issues or appointments which he has cited, provided that the limitations cited above are kept in mind. [8]

Using the above methods, a coding manual was prepared and
utilized to code the interview schedules obtained in the study.   Data
were then keypunched for machine tabulation, four cards being used
for each case.

To the greatest extent possible, the data were subjected to statistical tests of significance in order to prove or disprove the hypotheses of the investigation. Because of the nature of the data (for the most part nominal and ordinal), the nonparametric chi-square test of proportions was used for tests of significance.

Coding Reliability

In order to deal with the problem of coding reliability, a stratified random sample of 10 percent of the cases was chosen for coding by two other people who had not participated in the study in any way. No significant differences in interpreting the data were found, with such discrepancies as did occur being random in nature.

Notes

1. Criteria for exclusion were: first, if three-quarters of the top administrative officers and the head librarian were members of a formal religious order; second, if more than 25 percent of the faculty members of the college were members of a formal religious order. If a college met either criterion, it was dropped from the population. Twenty-two colleges, or 42 percent of those meeting the other criteria, were thus eliminated from the population.

2. Chicago: American Library Association, 1967.

3. Washington: Government Printing Office, 1967.

4. See Claire Selltiz et al., Research Methods in Social Relations (rev. ed.; New York: Holt, Rinehart & Winston, 1959), p. 241-243, regarding the relative merits of interviews versus questionnaires. See also Aaron V. Cicourel, Method and Measurement in Sociology (Glencoe, Ill.: Free Press, 1964), p. 73-104, for a theoretical discussion of interviewing.

5. The stratified random sampling of colleges for the main investigation was made prior to the choice of the two colleges for pretesting in order that all twenty-nine of the colleges in the population would have the opportunity of being chosen for the study.

6. A somewhat flexible time limitation was imposed to counteract the problem of faculty turnover and give what was hoped would be a limited degree of comparability in the choice of issues.

7.   Charles H. Backstrom and Gerald D. Hursh, Survey Research
     (Evanston, Ill.: Northwestern University Press, 1963), p.
     155.

8.   Selltiz et al., op. cit., p. 391-398, consider the problems of
     coding the relatively unstructured data obtained in open-
     ended questions.

BIBLIOGRAPHY

Abrahamson, Mark. The Professional in the Organization. Chicago: Rand McNally, 1967.

Backstrom, Charles H., and Gerald D. Hursh. Survey Research. Evanston, Ill.: Northwestern University Press, 1963.

Barber, Bernard. Social Stratification: A Comparative Analysis of Structure and Process. New York: Harcourt, Brace, 1957.

Bergen, Daniel P. "Librarians and the Bipolarization of the Academic Enterprise." College and Research Libraries, XXIV (November, 1963), 467-480.

Bergen Daniel P., and E.D. Duryea. Libraries and the College Climate of Learning. Syracuse: Syracuse University Press, 1964.

Blau, Peter M., and W. Richard Scott. Formal Organizations: A Comparative Approach. San Francisco: Chandler Publishing Company, 1962.

Branscomb, Harvie. Teaching with Books: A Study of College Libraries. Hamden, Conn.: The Shoe String Press, Inc., 1964.

Branscomb, Lewis C. "The Case for Faculty Status for Academic Librarians" Chicago: American Library Association, 1970.

Bundy, Mary Lee, and Paul Wasserman. "Professionalism Reconsidered." College and Research Libraries, XXIX (January, 1968), 5-26.

Cantril, Hadley. The Pattern of Human Concerns. New Brunswick, N.J.: Rutgers University Press, 1965.

Cicourel, Aaron V. Method and Measurement in Sociology. Glencoe, Ill.: Free Press, 1964.

Cochran, William G. Sampling Techniques. 2nd ed. New York: Wiley, 1963.

Dahl, Robert A. Who Governs? Democracy and Power in an American City. New Haven: Yale University Press, 1961.

Deale, H. Vail (ed.). "Trends in College Librarianship." Library Trends, XVIII (July, 1969).

Denis, Laurent Germain. "Academic and Public Librarians in Canada: A Study of the Factors which Influence Graduates of Canadian Library Schools in Making their First Career Decision in Favor of Academic or Public Libraries." Unpublished Ph. D. dissertation, Rutgers University, 1969.

Douglas, Robert R. "The Personality of the Librarian." Unpublished Ph. D. dissertation, University of Chicago, 1957.

Downs, Robert B. (ed.). The Status of American College and University Librarians. ACRL Monograph No. 22. Chicago: American Library Association, 1958.

Ennis, Philip H., and Howard W. Winger. Seven Questions about the Profession of Librarianship. Chicago: University of Chicago Press, 1962.

Etzioni, Amitai. Modern Organizations. Englewood Cliffs, N. J.: Prentice-Hall, 1964.

Festinger, Leon, and Daniel Katz. Research Methods in the Behavioral Sciences. New York: Holt, Rinehart and Winston, 1953.

Freund, John E. Modern Elementary Statistics. 3rd ed. Englewood Cliffs, N. J.: Prentice-Hall, 1967.

Fussler, Herman H. The Function of the Library in the Modern College. Chicago: University of Chicago Press, 1967.

Holbrook, Florence. "The Faculty Image of the Academic Librarian." Southeastern Librarian (Fall, 1968), p. 174-193.

Jencks, Christopher, and David Riesman. The Academic Revolution. Garden City, N. Y.: Doubleday, 1969.

Johnson, B. Lamar. Vitalizing the College Library. Chicago: American Library Association, 1939.

Jordan, Robert T. "Libraries of the Future for the Liberal Arts College." Library Journal, XCII (February 1, 1967), 537-539.

Knapp, Patricia B. College Teaching and the College Library. ACRL Monograph No. 23. Chicago: American Library Association, 1959.

_____. The Monteith College Library Experiment. New York: The Scarecrow Press, Inc., 1966.

_____. "The College Librarian: Sociology of a Professional
Specialization," in The Status of American College and University Librarians. Edited by Robert R. Downs. ACRL
Monograph No. 22. Chicago: American Library Association, 1958.

Lazersfeld, Paul F., and Wagner Thielens, Jr. The Academic
Mind: Social Scientists in a Time of Crisis. Glencoe, Ill.:
Free Press, 1958.

Liesener, James Will. "An Empirical Test of the Validity of the
Core Concept in the Preparation of University Librarians."
Unpublished Ph.D. dissertation, University of Michigan,
1967.

Library Statistics of Colleges and Universities, 1965-66. Institutional Data. Chicago: American Library Association, 1967.

Library Statistics of Colleges and Universities: Data for Individual
Institutions, Fall, 1968. Washington, D.C.: United States
Government Printing Office, 1969.

Lyle, Guy R. The Administration of the College Library. 3rd ed.
New York: H.W. Wilson Co., 1961.

Mayhew, Lewis B. The Smaller Liberal Arts College. New York:
The Center for Applied Research in Education, Inc., 1962.

Meyer, Donald P. "An Investigation of Perceptions Regarding the
Instructional Function of the Library among Faculty Members and Librarians at Public Community Colleges in Michigan." Unpublished Ph.D. dissertation, University of Michigan, 1968.

Miller, Delbert C. Handbook of Research Design and Social Measurement. New York: David McKay Co., Inc., 1964.

Morrison, Perry D. The Career of the Academic Librarian: A
Study of the Social Origins, Educational Attainments, Voca-
tional Experience, and Personality Characteristics of a
Group of American Librarians. Chicago: American Library
Association, 1969.

Nosow, Sigmund, and William H. Form (eds.). Man, Work, and
Society. New York: Basic Books, Inc., 1962.

Perreault, Jean. "What is Academic Status?" College and Research Libraries, XXVII (May, 1966), 207-210.

Plate, Kenneth Harry. "Middle Management in University Libraries: The Development of a Theoretical Model for Analysis."
Unpublished Ph.D. dissertation, Rutgers University, 1969.

142   Librarians and Decision Making

Randall, William M., and Francis Goodrich. Principles of College
    Library Administration. Chicago: University of Chicago
    Press, 1936.

Ryan, Mary Jane. "Librarians' Perceptions of Librarianship."
    Unpublished Ph.D. dissertation, University of Southern Cali-
    fornia, 1967.

Sanford, Nevitt (ed.). The American College: A Psychological and
    Social Interpretation of the Higher Learning. New York:
    John Wiley and Sons, Inc., 1962.

Scherer, Henry H. "Faculty-Librarian Relationships in Selected
    Liberal Arts Colleges." Unpublished Ed.D. dissertation,
    University of Southern California, 1960.

Schiller, Anita R. Characteristics of Professional Personnel in
    College and University Libraries. Springfield: Illinois State
    Library, 1969.

Seibert, Russell H. "Status and Responsibilities of Academic Li-
    brarians." College and Research Libraries, XXII (July,
    1961), 253-255.

Selltiz, Claire, et al. Research Methods in Social Relations. Re-
    vised ed. New York: Holt, Rinehart & Winston, 1959.

Selznick, Philip. TVA and the Grass Roots: A Study in the Soci-
    ology of Formal Organization. New York: Harper and Row,
    1966.

Shaffer, Dale Eugene. The Maturity of Librarianship as a Profes-
    sion. Metuchen, N.J.: The Scarecrow Press, Inc., 1968.

Shores, Louis, Robert Jordan, and John Harvey (eds.). The Li-
    brary-College: Contributions for American Higher Education
    at the Jamestown College Workshop, 1965. Philadelphia:
    Drexel Press, 1966.

Siegel, Sidney. Nonparametric Statistics for the Behavioral Sci-
    ences. New York: McGraw-Hill, 1956.

Simon, Herbert A. Administrative Behavior. 2nd ed. New York:
    The Free Press, 1957.

Swarthmore College. Critique of a College. Reports of the Com-
    mission on Educational Policy, the Special Committee on Li-
    brary Policy and the Special Committee on Student Life.
    Swarthmore, Pa.: Swarthmore College, 1967.

Weber, David C. "Tenure for Librarians in Academic Institutions."
    College and Research Libraries. XXVII (March, 1966), 99-
    102.

Whitten, Joseph N. "The Relationship of College Instruction to Libraries in 72 Liberal Arts Colleges." Unpublished Ed. D. dissertation, New York University, 1958.

Wilson, Logan. The Academic Man: A Study in the Sociology of a Profession. London: Oxford University Press, 1942.

Wilson, Louis R., and Maurice F. Tauber. The University Library. New York: Columbia University Press, 1956.